MAXIMIZING THE HUMAN POTENTIAL

UNLOCKING THE POWER WITHIN YOU

ANDREW SHAFFER

Copyright © 2017 Andrew Shaffer

All rights reserved.

No part of this work may be reproduced, or stored in a retrieval system, or transmitted in any form or by any means, electronic, mechanical, photocopying, recording, or otherwise without written permission of the author.

ISBN: 978-1543290851

CONTENTS

CHAPTER 1 - LESSONS LEARNED 1
    Jekel's Law of Human Dynamics 12
    "You're One of Those Guys" 15

CHAPTER 2 - THE MIND 19
    Training Your Subconscious 21
    Personal Paradigm 23
    Paradigm Shift 25
    Being in the Zone 28
    1950 US Open 31

CHAPTER 3 - VISION 33
    Dream 35
    Create the Vision 37
    Habit 46
    Having the Right Vision 48
    Vision and the Mind 50

CHAPTER 4 - LEADERSHIP 53
    Be Inspirational 56
    Be Humble 57
    Be Yourself 58
    Be Accessible 59
    Time Management 62

CHAPTER 5 - ATTITUDE 65
    Monday Morning 67
    Responding versus Reacting 68

Luck 72
Positive Thinking 74
Passion 75

CHAPTER 6 – BUILDING A TEAM 79
Identify Talent 81
Develop Talent 82
Mentoring 84
The "A" Team and "C" Team Myth 89
Hero Mentality 91
Shared Results 93

CHAPTER 7 – MAXIMIZE YOUR POTENTIAL 97
Develop Your Vision 100
Risk 102
Change Your Paradigms 104
Goals 105
Compensation 106
Continuous Improvement 108

CHAPTER 8 – MAXIMIZE THE POTENTIAL OF YOUR TEAM 111
Management Philosophy 112
Articulate Your Vision 115
Communicate Expectations 116
Treat Everyone with Respect 119
Loyalty 121
Engagement 124
Rewards 126
Accountability 127
Free Lunch 129

CHAPTER 9 – CHALLENGES 133
    Fear 134
    Overcoming the Paradigm 137
    Changing Cultures 138
    Status Quo 143

CHAPTER 10 – FIND YOUR PURPOSE 147
    Don't Limit Yourself 148
    Purpose 151
    Pride 152
    Karma 157
    Closing 157

DEDICATION

This book is dedicated to Yoko.
Without your love and support I would never have had the courage to chase my dreams! Thank you for everything you do!

INTRODUCTION

What do Apple, Microsoft, Netflix, Uber, and Southwest Airlines all have in common? They all redefined an industry and as a result became industry leaders. The iPhone, Windows OS, DVDs, and streaming videos delivered to your home, fast economic ride sharing, and low-fare air transportation with high reliability and friendly service. These have become the benchmarks for their respective industries. Companies like these, as well as the people who founded them are able to be successful despite any circumstances. They seem to weather any economic storm and are relatively unaffected by anything that is happening in the environment around them. The people leading these companies appear to have the Midas touch, where everything they do turns into gold.

There are others in those industries who are able to continue to progress toward their goals, slowly but surely, and are only somewhat impacted by their environment. Then there are those who seem to find life to be a struggle, and everywhere they turn something happens and they can't seem to catch a break.

No matter which of these categories resonates most with you, I have good news. This book is written for anyone that wants to see, or continue to see dramatic improvements toward reaching their professional or personal goals, in other words those that want to have the Midas touch with everything they do and want to be a leader in their field. The philosophies presented in this book are based on the idea that life is not a series of random events that happen, but a series of events that you cause to happen. By causing the events that happen to you in your life, by default you create the type of life you are living, whether it is beneficial or detrimental to your well-being. This is exciting because this means that we can change the events happening in our lives to create the results we want to see!

To understand that philosophy better you must realize that your results are a direct reflection of what is going on inside of you, in your mind. Until we change the inside, the way we think, the outside, our circumstances, are not going to change.

The results we produce in our lives are simply the results we know how to achieve, not necessarily the results we want. For example, if you are making $100,000 a year, you may want to make $200,000; the only thing holding you back is your awareness of how to make $200,000. At this point, it is likely that you are thinking; *I am not making $200,000 because my company won't pay me that much*. Well, you first have to learn to be aware of how to make more money, to improve your value, then do the things required to change your results. When you are providing $200,000 worth of service to your company they will pay you or risk losing you to a competitor that will.

For every action there is a reaction. This means whenever you take some action, any action, there is a reaction and we refer to these reactions as our result. Your action may be to go to work every day, and the result is a paycheck on Friday. A vast majority, you could say almost all, of what we do every day is done through habit. Our habits cause us to perform tasks, such as brushing our teeth, driving, and our daily work routines, without any conscious thought. Habits are good because they free our minds up so we don't have to concentrate on our daily routine. However, if our habits cause us to perform almost all of the actions in our day, if we want to have a permanent change in our results we have to change our habits.

To accomplish any goal that you have requires you to change what you are doing, and as your behaviors change your results will change. To make any long-lasting permanent changes to your behaviors and to consistently achieve the results you are looking to achieve you have to go to the root cause of behaviors, which is your habits—the things you do every day without any conscious thought. If you try to only change a behavior and not change the habit, the result will be temporary. This is exactly why so many people fail with their New Year's resolutions: they change behaviors without changing habits.

Most of us have spent a lifetime pursuing and accumulating knowledge. Most companies invest thousands of dollars (or more) in training their employees. We invest money in ourselves to accumulate more knowledge with the intent to make us more valuable. After all, knowledge is power, right? Wait; let's think about that. Do companies hire you for what you know or what you do? Perhaps an entry-level job will hire you for what you know, but as you become more experienced, promotions and opportunities are offered to those who "do," those who get results.

Oh, no! Why did I do that? I know better than that! Do these words sound familiar? If I had a dollar for every time I'd muttered those words, I would probably have enough to retire, but instead it seems at times I am destined to make the same mistakes over and over again. I do learn from them, as soon as I make the same mistake I immediately realize I know better, but that doesn't change the fact that I continue to do the same things and continue to get the same results. Obviously, at least for me, having knowledge doesn't necessarily mean that I will produce different results. The one example I always use: I know that if I allow myself to eat doughnuts in the morning or a piece of cake in the evening, I will not like the results. Yet I still allow myself the doughnut or piece of cake. I know that if I spend some extra time preparing for a presentation or a meeting with a client, I am more likely to make a sale, but I don't always do it. I know that if I want to be the best in my profession, I need to continuously study and learn so I can grow, yet I find myself watching mindless TV in the evenings. I am sure that I am not the only one who makes these same mistakes.

If you really want to chase after your desires, you will have to do things you've never done before, which will cause you to be uncomfortable. Change causes discomfort and like I said, to change your results you need to change your behaviors. You need to learn to be comfortable being uncomfortable. You will have to learn to do things that your peers are not doing. You will have to spend time reading or taking classes instead of watching TV. You will have to come in early to work, or stay late at night to prepare for that presentation or sales meeting. The good news is you can change, and if you read and learn from the information provided in this book, I promise you will be able to get what you want and more.

CHAPTER 1
Lessons Learned

For many years, starting with my career in the Navy and continuing as I worked my way up the engineering ranks and into management, I worked hard and that brought me to a certain level of success, although not to the level of success I wanted. The mistake I was making was to assume that my efforts would speak for themselves and my superiors would recognize my efforts and reward me with higher pay and promotions. It took me a while to realize how much control I had over my own destiny, and to realize that to achieve the level of success I wanted I could no longer continue to just work hard. Working hard and getting results is absolutely important, but that is not the only requirement to be successful. Continuing to work hard and working the same way only guaranteed that I would continue to do the same thing. The next level of responsibility that I was striving for required a different set of skills; therefore to be rewarded with the next promotion I had to start demonstrating those skills while in the position I had at the time. I had to raise my level of awareness and provide value above and beyond what my job description required.

After realizing that hard work alone would not necessarily cause me to achieve the level of success I was hoping to achieve, and the understanding that I needed to start demonstrating the skills required for the next position, I made the conscious decision to change the way I pursued success. I began by studying successful people, and I tried to learn from their actions and behaviors. I tried to understand what my boss's concerns were and thought of ways to help alleviate those concerns. I watched the people around me, listened to how leaders spoke, and read volumes of books on the topics of leadership, management, and the philosophies of success.

Shortly after getting promoted into management I found myself talking to a man, Robert Sullivan, who would later become an advisor and a mentor to me. Robert was my aunt's boyfriend at the time, a successful entrepreneur, and an expert in reviving struggling trucking companies. Robert started giving me tidbits of advice about being a good manager and the importance of leadership. He gave me a copy of a book he had written for leaders in the trucking business, so being a manager in the engineering field, I wasn't exactly his target audience, but the first part of the book focused on lessons in leadership and the lessons were universal. Shortly after reading Robert's book, he and I were at another family event and I took advantage of the opportunity to ask him questions about the contents of his book. I was extremely interested in his leadership theories and practices and I wanted to learn more than what was printed on the pages of his book. Robert then gave me a reading list of four additional books he recommended that I read. That following Monday I went to the bookstore, bought the four recommended books—*Think and Grow Rich* by Napoleon Hill, *The Master Key System* by Charles F. Haanel, *The Science of Getting Rich* by Wallace D. Wattles, and *The Secret* by Rhonda Byrne—and proceeded to read them all. Until this point I was not much of a reader, so this was a dramatic turning point in my life, and these books literally changed my life for the better. These books changed the way I thought, the way I approached problems, and my entire outlook on my purpose for living. These books taught me to stop waiting my turn and to go get whatever it is that I want. This was appealing to me because it is in harmony with my naturally ambitious and impatient temperament.

While I began to read and study the books Robert recommended, I made it a habit to keep a small notebook and a pencil with me. When I'd come across something that stimulated my thinking, I'd write it down. When I'd wake up in the middle of the night with an inspiration, I'd write it down. Eventually I began to reflect on all that I had written down, and what it all meant. I started thinking about what makes some people more successful and wondering why it can't happen to everyone. I theorized that success was more of a mindset than a specific talent or mere opportunity. After that realization I then considered how I could effectively use this new understanding to maximize my own potential and more importantly how I could help those around me maximize their own potential.

One of the fundamentals to being successful is being a good leader. Leaders are able to multiply their effectiveness by getting members of their team focused and working toward the same goal. As I reflected upon some leaders I had in the past, I looked to identify characteristics of leaders I admired and others that I was glad I no longer worked for. I wanted to see what characteristics I might want to employ in my own leadership style.

My first experience with good leadership and poor leadership was at a pizza place where I worked during high school, Pizza by Mama K. Most of the supervisors were just guys and girls that had worked there longer, but who had no real leadership experience. However, even in this relatively inexperienced work force we all knew who the good leaders were. On weeknights the restaurant closed at 11:30, and as usual with most retail businesses before we were able to close we had to have everything clean, so all of the dishes had to be washed, floors mopped, and prep areas sanitized. I can remember that Rob was a supervisor that got us out of the door at 11:35, unless there was a last-minute delivery and then we would all be waiting until that last driver returned to the store. Rob would have his closing paperwork completed, the store cleaned, and everyone finished delivering pizzas at closing time. We all liked working for Rob, because we knew what time we were leaving work. Conversely there was another supervisor that would struggle to get us out the door an hour after closing. We had to spend that extra time cleaning, while he was finishing up his paperwork. Now, I did get paid to stay there for an extra hour, at something like $5.25 per hour, and there were typically about four of us, so it cost the store around $21 more for the inefficiency of each of his shifts. Probably not breaking the bank, but a clear example, in my mind, of the difference a good leader makes. We all liked working for Rob—not that we didn't like working for the other supervisors—but there was something different when Rob worked that seemed to make the place run more smoothly. On Rob's shifts there seemed to be more energy and efficiency. I eventually grew in my responsibility to become a supervisor, and at one point I even ran one of the restaurant branches. When I was in a leadership position I tried to model my teams after the way that Rob ran his teams: with energy and efficiency.

Later, while in the Navy and stationed in Japan I had the privilege of working for Petty Officer First Class Swank. Petty Officer Swank was an interesting guy. Swank was from the Philippines, and at the time most of the Filipinos worked either in the galley or supply chain. Petty Officer Swank started his career as an unrated airman, which means he was not assigned to a tech school after boot camp. Early in his Navy career Petty Officer Swank wanted to be an aviation electronics technician (AT). Being an AT required an understanding of advanced electronic theory, so it was often challenging for someone to learn it without being accepted into tech school. When Petty Officer Swank passed the exam to become an AT, he was told that he would never make it past the rank of E-4. Petty Officer Swank had a vision of himself and for his capabilities and therefore refused to believe that his potential was limited. When I worked with Petty Officer Swank he was an E-6, two promotions past an E-4, and I have been told that he continued to be promoted during his career.

Petty Officer Swank ran a very productive shop. Swank showed leadership, and a genuine desire to be successful and improve his performance as well as that of those on his team. As a result those of us on his team would do anything he asked, and would give that extra discretionary effort when working with him. Going the extra mile was not something we thought about, at least I didn't, but we would do it because we wanted to. You can be assured that as a junior enlisted sailor some of the jobs we were asked to do were less than desirable, but they all needed to be done. Members of Petty Officer Swank's team never felt like we were being picked on or singled out; it was part of the job. Eventually Petty Officer Swank was moved to the Quality Assurance shop and we got a new lead petty officer for our shop. The new guy was a decent man; however he was content to just do his job and didn't have that natural drive to improve the productivity of the shop. As a result he didn't command the same respect that Petty Officer Swank had, nor did he possess the natural leadership ability that Swank demonstrated, and as a result productivity went down.

Petty Office Swank clearly had a vision of how he wanted his career to go. He did not accept the stereotype that Filipinos would work in the galley or supply chain, and challenged that by taking and passing the AT exam. Petty Office Swank clearly demonstrated strong and proficient leadership and management skills, demonstrated by the decline in shop production after he rotated to Quality Assurance. Finally Swank didn't have the advantage of seven months of tech school to learn his trade, and had to put in the time to study through on the job training and through other material available to him. By taking the initiative to learn his skill and overcome his perceived hurdles Swank clearly took action to execute a plan that enabled him to complete a successful Navy career, much more successful than it would have been if he had not had the determination to succeed after being told he would not be able to advance past the rank of E-4.

By the time my enlistment was almost over, I had gotten married and was half contemplating a career in the Navy. With only a few months left on my enlistment I had found a way to reinjure a shoulder that I initially hurt playing high school football. The Navy doctor said I would need some physical therapy and further evaluation to determine if surgery would be required. The squadron was about to go to sea, meaning that to receive the recommended physical therapy I would be permitted to stay back and not go to sea. I talked to the commanding officer (CO) to explain my situation, and he agreed that I could stay behind. I thought I was getting treated well by my CO and the Navy so I put in the paperwork to extend my enlistment for two months. Extending my enlistment for two months would provide me the opportunity to entertain potential shore duty back in the states, which could provide some stability considering I had just gotten married. Well, shortly after the CO made a deal with me, there was a change of command. The incoming CO did not honor the promise of the outgoing CO—I was going to sea. No physical therapy. No further evaluation to determine if surgery was necessary. I was extremely upset so I immediately submitted the paperwork to separate at the end of my enlistment while my original request to extend was still in the approval cycle. As required I went to sea, I did the bare minimum, and probably less than that. I was actively disengaged the entire time. Within weeks I went from considering a career in the Navy to an attitude of "get me out of here." The difference was solely based on the way I was treated by the squadron leadership.

After the Navy I went to college and received a bachelor's degree in engineering. Immediately after graduating I landed a job in Houston, Texas, working on the space shuttle program. I went there as part of the hiring they did to get the space shuttles back in flight after the space shuttle *Columbia* accident in February 2003. The people I worked with were a real close group of people, and I still visit some of them from time to time. The team I worked with generally cared for each other and would all pull together when someone needed help. A lot of the things we'd help each other with were outside of work activities, such as when someone was moving, having a kid, or needed a hand with a home project.

One specific example of when we all pulled together was in the fall of 2005. There was a Category 5 hurricane, Hurricane Rita, coming straight to Galveston Bay. This was the one scenario that was highly likely to wipe out my house, and really most of the people I worked with were in the same situation. To help put this in context, this was a few weeks after Hurricane Katrina devastated New Orleans. There had been significant damage and looting after Hurricane Katrina, which was obviously fresh in all of our minds. To further complicate matters my wife was nine months pregnant with our first child, and on strict orders to avoid stress, drink lots of water, and eat. Real good timing for her! In an effort to support each other my coworkers and I all pulled together. Several of us dispersed to different hardware stores to buy whatever plywood we could find. As you can probably imagine plywood was in high demand and short supply; therefore we were a traveling band of guys going out and helping each other board up our windows and secure valuables. I don't really remember anyone asking for help; it was more along the lines of "Hey, I'll come over to your house to help you get your house ready. Great, after that we'll go to your house." This was an example where we all honestly cared about each other, and we were willing to go that extra mile to make sure we were all prepared for the storm.

My wife and I planned to evacuate after securing our belongings, and a colleague and neighbor invited my wife and me to his parents' house for the storm, where his parents made it a mission to spoil my wife! We just took care of each other, which was what we did. This experience taught me the value of building teams or in this case building a strong community of friends that were genuinely concerned with each other's well-being.

Leaving that job was one of the hardest things I ever did. If we really looked out for each other, why did I leave? The short answer—my boss. I learned a lot from him as well. His office was probably no more than 10 feet away from my cube, and he never talked to me. He would conduct weekly staff meetings where we would have an opportunity to tell him what we were working on, and I do not believe he fully appreciated the tasks the members of his team were working on. Nor do I believe he ever spent any effort to get to know his direct reports. These are behaviors I vowed I would never do when I became a manager. There can be a thousand reasons someone does not want to work with me, but lacking access will not be one of them, PERIOD.

Toward the end of my tenure there, my boss put out a task list for the next few years. It was the plan for our special projects and shuttle flight assignments. When I looked at the assignments I quickly noticed I had about a two-year period where I had nothing assigned to me. Being a young engineer, and by nature someone that wants to contribute when I go to work in the morning, I decided I would ask him about this gap and see if there was something else that I could help with. I walked into his office and brought up my concern. His response, and I quote: "Don't worry about it." That was not very comforting. So I started applying for new jobs, and eventually found one. At this point in my career I was not familiar with the theory that people do not quit their jobs, they quit their bosses. I fully believe this now, as I know I have changed jobs more than once because I wanted to get away from a particular boss. Having a great team to work with does not offset poor leadership.

Eventually I finally had the opportunity to lead a team. I was leading an engineering team responsible for integrating and testing products for the project I was assigned to. In addition to the integration and test responsibilities, I was also responsible for the field engineering work as well. During this time the engineering manager received a call from the customer asking for support to resolve a problem in the field with one of our delivered products. Getting the product operational was important to the customer because they had to accomplish some specific testing tied to important program milestones. In other words, big money was at stake. At this time, we really didn't have scope in our contract to allow us to do this work, but our program director made the decision to take the high road and directed us to help our customer meet their program needs.

There was little data available to us to help us understand what the problem was; therefore we did not know exactly what skill set was needed to effectively resolve the issue. Fortunately, the field site where the investigations took place was close enough that it was only a few hours' drive, and I could shuffle people around if my initial team decided they needed more or different support. However, as with all unplanned and out-of-scope work, I wasn't necessarily staffed to meet this additional workload. Also I already had a busier than normal week that was going to stress my staff. We had hardware backed up that needed to be tested and shipped to make our contract delivery date, and we were required to meet a software delivery as well. Most weeks with a full staff this type of workload would be hard to handle, and now I needed to send people to the field. Not only was I sending people to the field, I had to send my best and most versatile engineers to the field, and therefore I had to rely on my bench strength to meet the demanding schedules in the plant.

After the engineering manager made the request for support and asked what I could do, I met with the members of my team and I explained the situation. I asked my most versatile team members if they could travel, and what they thought they would need for support from the office. I explained to my staff that those of us not going to the field would have to step up and fill in for those team members going out of town. Before I could fully develop my plan for executing all of our tasks back at home, I had people coming up to me and saying that they could stay late and help with this testing or that activity. These people were offering to go the extra mile, to put in that discretionary effort needed to ensure team success, and I didn't have to ask anyone.

As a rule I tried to maintain a bench strength of about 1.5 deep, meaning people were familiar with the other team members' jobs but were not necessarily proficient in fulfilling these roles. Now these guys were being challenged to step up and take a lead role. They had to fill in for the starters. Every one of them took the initiative to learn whatever they needed to do to get their jobs done, and they accomplished all three tasks and did not miss a delivery. I did not have to direct or dictate to anyone to do anything; they all stepped up to get the job done. The program director was proud of the guys that helped the customer, and I was equally as proud of the guys that kept the wheels moving back at the plant. I knew what they had done, and it was just as impressive.

The success of both the field team and the team that remained in the office was not caused by happenstance or dumb luck. From my experience evacuating from Hurricane Rita while living in Houston, I knew the value of having teammates, or friends, available to help when needed. Therefore from the moment I took over as a team leader I stressed the importance of working together, and being there when someone on the team needs help. I presented a vision of where the team would be working as one combined unit toward a common goal, and when this theory was challenged, my team stepped up without hesitation and they were able to overcome any and all obstacles before them.

Jekel's Law of Human Dynamics

At one point in my career I was working at a rather large company with a variety of products and services as well as multiple campuses spread around the world. It was while in this position that I had the opportunity to lead a group that was going through some tough times. The campus I was working at had just lost a few key proposals, so work was getting thin and as a result people were getting reassigned to other locations or taking any assignment that was available. This was a challenging time for everyone involved. The individual contributors struggled because they didn't know how long they would have jobs. The management struggled because we had to make some tough decisions and we worked frantically to avoid laying anyone off.

We reached our bottom while approaching the end of the year, and before I left for the holidays, I reflected on what could be done to help change the trajectory and improve our workload. The general conversation in the hallway typically blamed the front office, and the company executives that the front office reported to, and yes, there was some blame to be placed there. However, I believed there were things that we could all do to help improve our success rate for proposal capture and even improve our performance on existing contracts. Over the holiday break, I really thought about what could be done, and after the break, I laid out a vision for both the leadership teams and for my direct reports. The key to my vision was strong leadership with a focus on improving morale. I believed that if the leadership allowed the circumstances to result in a victim mentality, we would just perpetuate a further decline. I challenged everyone to look at themselves and their teams to see where they could become more effective in their jobs. It was all of our responsibility, not just the front office's, to ensure success in everything we do, from executing on existing programs to developing innovative and cost-effective solutions for our customers. Every member of every team has some responsibility in these areas.

During these times I realized the importance of maintaining and actually improving the morale of my team. I started writing motivational quotes on a whiteboard on the wall in my office to remind me and all those that came into my office the importance of staying positive and being focused on making changes that will change the trajectory of our business captures. These quotes would become conversation starters when people entered my office and eventually members of my team started to add their own thoughts to the board. One thought in particular stood out and I would often find myself pondering its meaning. An engineer named Mark Jekel wrote the following on my whiteboard:

Jekel's Law of Human Dynamics
"Humans are 75% water, and 75% of the time will, like water, take the path of least resistance."

When Mark wrote this on my board, it was clear to me that in order to turn around the trajectory of our campus we could no longer afford to take the path of least resistance. The path of least resistance was to blame the front office and continue to do things the way they had always been done. If that worked, we wouldn't have been facing the situation we were facing. We had to fight the path of least resistance and become more innovative and creative in our execution and performance.

Over the next year, with a focus on improving morale and exploring new ways to conduct our business, the campus slowly began to become more successful in securing work and executing on existing programs. Within a few months the campus won two major contracts; one of them was unexpected and work started coming in and the management team went from worrying about employment for our current staff to actively looking to bring on additional staff to accomplish the increased workload.

Jekel's Law of Human Dynamics was more than a slogan to help my team through some tough times: I really like that statement because to me it was a way to explain the characteristics that the highly successful people in our society demonstrate compared to those who are less successful. When I talk about success I am not necessarily talking about money, although money generally follows success. I am talking about living a life that is truly rewarding. I have come to believe, through research and experience, that those who have a habit of taking the path of least resistance are not the people who live extraordinary lives. Individuals who are always looking for a get-rich-quick scheme, or find it easier to accept the status quo in their own life, are not the individuals who have achieved the highest levels of success in their lives. Those who take on the challenges life presents, those who venture down the more difficult paths and take risks, will be rewarded for it.

Many times in my life I have had to weigh the benefits of taking the path of least resistance versus grinding it out and taking on a challenge, and one example of that was to pursue a skill and an education. I was not a disciplined student in my high school years, nor were many of my friends. I did not take advantage of the educational opportunities presented to me, and after graduation from high school I found myself without a marketable skill. Upon realizing that I needed a skill in order to improve my condition in life I decided to join the US Navy, which of course taught me several skills. After the Navy and with the encouragement of my wife I eventually wised up and got a college education to compliment the skills I learned in the Navy. I firmly believe that my life is better now than it would have been if I had not found the courage to take action, to resist the path of least resistance by enlisting in the Navy, and pursuing an education.

"You're One of Those Guys"

One evening, shortly after arriving at my first duty station in the Navy, I was probably overly confident for a variety of reasons and I blurted out that within six months I would be the best technician in my shop. There was no doubt about it, in my mind I would be the best, but being the "best" was completely subjective.

I worked second shift in my shop and second shift is primarily where the maintenance actions took place so the aircraft would be available to support flight operations the following day. When the flight crew would return from a flight, if there was a system that was not working appropriately they would write up a "gripe." Most of the gripes would be addressed on second shift because there were typically fewer flights during the second shift that would interfere with the maintenance actions. I may not have been the best in the shop within six months, but certainly within a year I was one of the better technicians, and by the time my enlistment was over, I would say I was the best. I measured that based on the numbers of "gripes" I would resolve each shift. Each night we were typically divided into four or five two-man teams and after every shift I counted how many gripes were signed off and my goal was to do 50% of the workload each night. If the shop fixed 30 gripes, I wanted to have signed off 15 of them. I want to be clear, that I didn't do all the work by myself, however, regardless of who was on my team we still managed to come close to the 50% mark on a regular basis.

One evening I was trying to give one of my shipmates some mentoring on how to perform a specific task and I was trying to make it less intimidating by simplifying the process. His response, and I remember what he said to this day: "It is easy for you because you're one of those guys." I didn't understand what he meant so I had to ask him what he meant by "one of those guys," to which he responded, "one of those guys that everything is easy." There are probably many reasons that my technician duties were easy for me, or at least perceived that way, but those words still stick in my head after almost 20 years. I can't really remember what we were doing at this time, but I do remember what my shipmate said to me.

The main thing is I had a vision of myself being the best technician in my shop, I made a decision that I was going to be the best in the shop, and I took action to realize this vision. I have provided data that supports my claim that I was one of the best in the shop. There is nothing special about me: I didn't grow up privileged, I have no superhuman talents, I just had a vision of where I wanted to go and I was determined to meet a goal.

So if I could excel as an aviation electronics technician, why not in other areas? I believe that we can all achieve much more than most of us believe we can. The majority of the people I have met do not believe they are "one of those guys" and as a result they don't put in the effort needed to achieve that high level of success. I believe that everyone can and should be "one of those guys."

So let me start this book with a challenge: are you someone for whom everything comes easy? If not, do you want to be? Do you want to live the type of life that has the appearance that everything comes easy to you?

CHAPTER 2
The Mind

DOCTORS WHO STUDY the brain will tell you that the human brain effectively has two parts. I've heard them referred to as "modern and primitive brains" or the "conscious and subconscious brain." The modern or conscious brain is responsible for rational thought and the primitive or subconscious brain is responsible for your emotional side and houses your instincts and habits.

The subconscious brain is the part of the brain that we've had since the beginning of time and requires no experience or education to function. The subconscious brain is responsible for maintaining body functions and our survival instincts. This part of the brain is designed to give you the inherent fear of fire, drowning, or predatory animals. It is what allows us to stand without concentrating on our balance. The subconscious brain is where the fight or flight instinct is contained and causes us to sweat when we are nervous. The subconscious brain is always active because it is responsible for keeping you alive; it controls your breathing, heartbeat, and organ function, which are obviously needed even when we sleep when the conscious brain is not active.

The conscious brain takes more energy to use, and is the area responsible for active thought. When we are born the conscious brain is a blank slate and is developed through our experiences and education. This is the part of the brain that we use when studying, working, or solving problems. This is the part of the brain that does everything that the subconscious brain does not. It is fortunate that there are two separate parts of the brain responsible for different functions. Imagine a time when you had a really mentally challenging day. Maybe it was a big meeting at work, or finals at school. These things use your conscious brain, and can drain your energy. I know I have personally gotten home from work and been so mentally exhausted I couldn't carry on a simple conversation with my wife or remember trivial things like my email passwords. Now, imagine if I still had to concentrate on breathing or keeping my heart beating. On days like that we literally could not survive—we would die of mental exhaustion.

If I was so mentally exhausted that I could no longer concentrate on simple tasks, how did I have the capability to drive myself home? Surely driving a car isn't something that our subconscious or "primitive" mind would know how to do. Driving is not something that is required for natural survival. That is correct, and herein lies the key. Your subconscious mind can be taught, and when your subconscious mind is taught a habit is formed. Habit, through the subconscious mind, is a gift that allows us to continuously do more tasks without expending the energy required to accomplish these tasks using our conscious mind. When you learned how to drive, I am sure it took more of your conscious mind, and over time driving became a habit. When you get a new job, or move houses, you use more of your conscious mind to find your route to work or the grocery store, but after a while, you can drive there without much thought at all. Your subconscious mind takes over.

Training Your Subconscious

Because we know that habits such as driving are programmed into your subconscious brain, it is now apparent that your subconscious can be trained. You might now be asking to what extent can it be trained, and how do we do it. I am here to tell you that it can be infinitely trained, and it is easy. Your subconscious is trained by repetitive thought and visualization from your conscious mind. When you repetitively visualize the same thing, you will begin to record that image into your subconscious. Your subconscious will then begin to develop the habits and instincts you need to be successful in attaining your goal: it's that simple.

Your subconscious mind is completely deductive, and can only accept what the conscious mind impresses upon it. When a person observes their outside circumstances and accepts those conditions as reality, the subconscious mind then takes that information and produces habits and actions that produce those same results. We have to accept that our habits and our paradigms are a type of mental programming. This programing can be intentional or unintentional. Without understanding of how the brain functions we are apt to look at our outside conditions and accept them as reality. We allow our outside circumstances to define who we are.

Over the years I have found that the majority of the people I have worked with are accustomed to receiving relatively the same merit increase year after year. It would fluctuate slightly year over year, but the increases would be in the same general ballpark. We were conditioned to believe that the merit increase was reasonable, and logically that made some sense. An increase of 5%–10% each year is logical and dramatic improvements of 100% or 200% are illogical. However, we have all been exposed to someone that has experienced these dramatic changes in income or success and when this happens we generally explain it as luck or ascribe some other reason why this happened. When we expect small incremental progress, we will receive small incremental progress. Our thoughts and actions will guide us to produce the results that we expect.

When you want to experience dramatic changes in your life, whether it be your income, lifestyle, contribution to society, or improved relationships, you have to be able to visualize, and become emotionally involved with a vision of what you are trying to achieve. Because your subconscious mind is completely deductive and can only accept what the conscious mind impresses upon it, the subconscious mind cannot differentiate between real and imagined. By imagining the end result of the goal that you desire to achieve and becoming emotionally involved with that end goal, that idea gets implanted into your subconscious mind and your conditioning or your programming begins to change.

To become whatever it is you want to become, that idea has to be seeded into your subconscious mind. When you decided to learn to drive, you had to practice over and over. I know in my case there were times I'd be driving with my father and he'd be hitting an imaginary brake, but over time I became better and he was able to relax in the car. Athletes will practice over and over hitting, throwing, running, etc., and a big part of their preparation is to visualize hitting harder, throwing better, or running faster. Actors will become mentally involved with the characters they will portray to make the character more lifelike. Whenever anyone prepares for an interview or a big meeting and imagines the questions they might be asked or rehearses their material to present, this is a type of visualization. The more repetition that you can perform, either physical or mental, the stronger that conditioning or programming becomes and those habits begun in your subconscious mind begin to produce the results you envision.

Personal Paradigm

Your personal paradigm is the collection of thoughts and ideas that are contained in your subconscious mind. Your paradigm defines who you are and how you interpret what is happening in the world around you. In order to expand your expectations in life (i.e., maximize your potential), you must overcome the limitations in your mind that are caused by the paradigm. Throughout our lives, starting from the day we are born, we discover the world through experimentation and develop our own instinctual guides for living in this world. We discover what scents appeal to us, what textures we find soothing, what we like to eat and drink. Even 40 years later when I am presented with a foreign concept I try to put it in the context of something I know. For example, I have worked on several different projects during my engineering career. Although some of the projects were relatively similar in technology and scope, they were all unique. On every project I tried to apply the principles and rules that were true for one project to the next. Often I would recognize I was doing this and I'd preface my comments with something along the lines of "From my experience on project A, I think this should be true on project B."

I would do this to point out where my reference point is coming from, and I am clearly saying that I see reality through this lens and if I need to alter my perception of reality please help me understand where my thought is flawed. The lens through which you interpret reality is your personal paradigm.

It is common for people to have trouble grasping, or even recognizing, a reality other than the one they understand. That really frustrates me, because it limits their own success and ability to reach their full potential. They see reality through their own lens and when presented with a situation that doesn't fit their paradigm, the ideas are either dismissed or rationalized using the rules set up in their personal paradigms. Worse yet is when we use our paradigm for an excuse to accept the status quo and not strive to reach our full potential. People will rationalize or make excuses like:

- I grew up in a rough neighborhood; therefore I can't amount to anything.
- My mother was an alcoholic; therefore I was neglected as a child and I can't do the things that others can.
- I don't know who my father is; I had no positive male influence in the home.
- I've always been poor; therefore I will always be poor.

Those examples are just excuses and limitations placed on your life by you through your own paradigm. All of these excuses are a result of the paradigms that were programmed in the mind, and the good news is these programs can be overwritten.

I've often said there are three sides to every story: yours, mine, and the truth. This is due to the realities that everyone sets for themselves through their paradigm. I have a reality and a series of events that happed in my life that were defined for me through the prism of my reality. The same is true for your side of the story. No two people have the same set of life experiences, so therefore no two sets of realities, or truths if you will, will be the same.

Once you recognize that your perception of reality is shaped by your personal experiences, and that truths can be a matter of perception, then—and only then—you can learn to expand your vision. When you expand your vision this is the point when you can begin to change your life.

Paradigm Shift

Many times when I am mentoring someone who desires more success in their profession I begin by asking that person to describe their professional goals. By the time these individuals begin working with me they are generally familiar with the idea of goal setting and how to achieve goals. At one time I was talking to a potential client, Matt, and I started asking him about his professional goals. Matt was already familiar with setting and achieving goals. He had been doing this for most of his life and had been successful. He is a former college football player and achieved a doctorate degree. Matt has also been relatively successful in his career because he understood the basics of goal setting and achieving. Because of the relative success Matt had achieved this far in his life he didn't think he really needed my services but agreed to continue working with me.

When I asked Matt about his professional goal, he was able to articulate a clear and detailed 5- to 10-year plan. Matt had identified what types of assignments he would have to accomplish and how long he'd have to stay at each rung of the success ladder. Matt obviously had a goal and a plan. My response to him was quite simple: what is it you want to do? Not the job title, but what do you want to do? When he thought about that he articulated something slightly different. I challenged Matt to go after that, instead of pursuing a laundry list of assignments he needed to accomplish. When I did this I challenged Matt's paradigm. He would counter my challenge with "That is not the way things are done." Or "It doesn't work that way." Matt's paradigm had him conditioned to believe that it would take him 10 years to reach his goal, and that there was a certain path to get where he wanted to go.

While working with Matt, I gave him exercises designed to change his paradigm. They are designed to help him think about what he really wants and to objectively evaluate the paradigms that were holding him back. Matt eventually saw how his paradigm was holding him back and he made a decision that he would try to accelerate his results. Matt walked into his boss's office and asked to be put in for a promotion. You may be able to imagine how well this went; you see, Matt's paradigm and conditioning was based upon what he observed in his organization, which means everyone in his organization thought the same way. When Matt asked for the promotion his boss responded by pointing out the relatively short span of time since his last promotion, and that he had only about half the years of experience typical of this type of promotion. Matt then challenged his boss's paradigm and made a compelling argument for the promotion until his boss finally agreed to push the promotion up the chain.

The resistance didn't stop at the next level, though. When the promotion package hit he next level of approval, the decision makers there had the same reaction. Their paradigms were expecting candidates that had a specific number of years' experience, and Matt still had only half of that. Fortunately for Matt he armed his boss with the information he needed so that his boss was able to plead the case and Matt eventually was promoted. This was a big promotion for Matt and allowed him to be eligible for a larger leadership position.

Shortly after the promotion, Matt was still working toward what he wanted, and not necessarily working within the confines of his previous paradigm, nor the paradigms of his organization. Matt saw that there was a management role open, and he asked his boss if he could fill that vacancy. This type of leadership role was generally filled with someone with twice Matt's experience, but Matt decided he should be considered for filling that vacancy. However, in order to be considered for this leadership role, Matt still had to face the paradigms of the hierarchy of his organization. Every step of the way he met with the same question and resistance, all focused on the paradigm that Matt needed a certain number of years before he could do the job. Never mind the fact that Matt met all other qualifications, except for the one he had no control over, which is time. Eventually Matt was able to convince his leadership team that he was the right person for the job, and he was given a team of his own to manage. By employing a simple change in his paradigm, Matt was able to accelerate a career progression that was planned to happen in 5 to 10 years into weeks. Yes, Matt accomplished this within weeks of changing his paradigm.

Being in the Zone

When I was a kid, I played little league baseball like most of the boys did in my hometown. I played from the summer I was 8 until the summer I was 13. After my games my mother would ask me if I heard something she yelled to me while I was playing. She would ask me this game after game, and the answer was always the same: I did not hear what she was saying. I didn't hear my own mother's voice, the voice that I had been conditioned to hear above all other voices, but during a game my mind was elsewhere. My subconscious mind was in control while I was playing, I was playing through habit.

In high school, I played a little football. I was the quarterback on a team that didn't have a very strong offensive line. I specifically remember at one point, the defensive nose tackle was grabbing my ankle as I was coming out from under the center. For those not completely familiar with football, this means the defensive player was getting past the guys who were supposed to be protecting me before I even had a chance to take a step back. Needless to say, I wouldn't have much time to get set for a pass or let a complicated play develop before I was running or getting hit by a defensive player.

When I was playing, my father would typically walk along the field staying level with me and watching the action. After the game he would ask me questions like, "How did you stand there to throw that pass with that linebacker running at you like that?" Another question he liked to ask was, "How did you know to take that step forward as the pocket was collapsing and make that pass?" My answer to him was, "I didn't know I did that." I was completely focused on executing the play. Again, my subconscious mind was in control while I was playing; I was playing through habit.

Now I golf, where there is significantly less chance of getting hurt than in baseball or football. When I golf, I have a pre-shot routine. I do the same thing every time before I hit the ball. When I start my routine, my goal is to become unaware of just about everything except the ball and the shot I am trying to execute. If something distracts me I have to back off and start the routine over again. The purpose of this routine is to allow my subconscious mind to take control while I execute my shot.

Finally, I've spoken to many people who have given speeches in front of large audiences or to senior members of their organizations. The people I spoke with are not typically the kinds of people who are accustomed to making presentations to these types of audiences. There is a common theme in all the stories: when they finished the presentation, none of them could remember what he had said. They got up, started the speech they had practiced and prepared, and entered their own world until it was all over. This is a type of extreme concentration.

In each of these cases, there is a reason I am unaware of my mother's voice, a linebacker, my buddies heckling me before I hit a golf shot, or not remembering the details of delivering an important speech. In common terms I am in a "zone." Being in the zone is when your subconscious brain is in charge, and your conscious brain is not directly involved in the activity. It's the same thing as when you drive into work and park your car and think to yourself, "I don't remember driving here." You obviously drove to work, and hopefully you did it safely, but you weren't concentrating on it, and you did it automatically. You drove to work by habit.

When I was a member of a sports team, our teams practiced several times a week. The purpose of this was to get the routines of the plays into our subconscious minds. Ironically these activities are referred to as muscle memory, but in reality muscles do not have any memory and the memory is being stored in your subconscious brain. While playing baseball as a young boy, I was doing what I was trained to do through repeated practice. During the games my subconscious mind was in control, and because of that my conscious mind was not; therefore I did not recognize things outside of what my training had taught me to recognize. When you think about it, while batting you don't have time to consciously think as a baseball is pitched. You don't say, "Wow that's coming at me pretty fast, maybe it's a fastball. I see some spin on it, so maybe it'll break. It might be outside the strike zone, so I won't swing." No, you make the decision to swing or not much faster than that. Your body makes the decision almost as soon as the ball leaves the pitcher's hand. Your subconscious mind recognizes the pattern almost immediately and a decision to swing and where to swing is made. Now, your subconscious mind isn't perfect and some people are better than others at recognizing the patterns that will determine where a pitch is going to go, and that is why we don't all play professional baseball.

When playing golf, the purpose of my pre-shot routine is to trigger my subconscious mind to take over during my swing. There are so many aspects of the golf swing that if I had to consciously think about keeping my elbow straight, shifting my weight from one leg to the other, rotating my hips, I would not be able to hit the ball well because it would be too much for the conscious mind to handle. When I am struggling in my game, typically it is because I allow my conscious mind to take over, and as a result I start thinking of the mechanics of my swing while swinging and end up making the game worse.

1950 US Open

Ben Hogan was a famous golfer in the middle of the 20th century. In the 1950 US Open, Hogan was in need of a par on the 72nd hole to force himself into a three-way playoff. Just to be in this position is a remarkable feat, because just a year prior Hogan was in a car accident that nearly took his life. Hogan finds himself 213 yards away from the green, and he hits a miraculous one-iron shot to the center of the green, makes par to get into the playoff, and eventually wins the playoff to win the US Open. Merion Golf Course, just outside of Philadelphia, where this tournament was played, still has a marker where Hogan made that shot, and professional golfers will still drop a ball there to mimic the famous shot.

Interestingly enough, Ben Hogan wrote about this shot in his book *Five Lessons*, but in his memory it wasn't nearly as miraculous as history remembers. Hogan said there was not anything spectacular about that particular shot; it was the same shot he had made thousands of times on the practice range. Hogan programmed his subconscious mind and body to make that shot. So when it came time to execute during that tournament, he executed flawlessly.

I can't get into Hogan's head, or possibly know what he was thinking at this time. I only know what he has said after the fact. Hogan had practiced this shot, and when he was in the game situation, his habit, his subconscious mind, did not allow the pressure of the moment to get in the way of executing the perfect shot when he needed to make it.

CHAPTER 3
Vision

THE MOST IMPORTANT part of achieving success is having a vision. A vision defines what it is you are trying to accomplish and provides a picture for the mind to work toward. When we are creating a vision, something that is extraordinary, we have to believe we can achieve whatever we imagine in our vision. We cannot achieve something unless we believe we can achieve it. If you think about this for a second, if you are trying to attain something and you do not fully believe you can achieve it, then the first time you meet an obstacle or a setback you will give up on your vision and rationalize it as "I knew I couldn't do that." So before creating your vision you have to examine your belief system. Do you have a strong foundation for your beliefs, and is what you believe accurate?

Let's examine a popular belief that an education is the key to success. Is this a sound belief and is there evidence to back up that claim? Since our early years in school we've all been told that to be successful, we need to graduate high school and go to college. We have been raised to believe that we need to study and learn this material so we can get a good job when we grow up. We spend countless hours and many years of our lives working to accumulate knowledge with the intention of improving our quality of life. When we get degrees we frame them and hang them on the wall, or put them on our resume to impress other people with how much we know. After all, if knowledge is power then knowing stuff leads to success.

However, there is no guarantee that getting educated will ensure that you will get a job. Listen to the news: the biggest challenge with young people today is they graduate college with a mountain of debt and move back in with their parents because they can't get a good job. There are literally thousands of educated people that are either unemployed or underemployed. Why? They went to school, they got their degrees and in many cases advanced degrees, they did everything right. What happened? They believed that getting an education would lead to a good job and that simply is not the case.

In NO WAY am I stating, implying, or insinuating that anyone should not get an education. I have a master's degree, and I expect that my kids will attend college. I firmly believe that being educated does give certain advantages. However, I do not believe that a good education is the key to success.

We all have known someone that was absolutely brilliant. Someone that has accumulated a lifetime of knowledge but they aren't able to translate that into success. We might say that they lack "street smarts" or they only have "book smarts" and "book smarts" don't necessarily translate into success.

Additionally, if we believed that being educated and getting a degree leads to success, then being uneducated would mean certain failure or eliminate the ability to get a good job. We also know this is not true. Dave Thomas was a high school dropout when he founded the Wendy's hamburger chain. Although it is worth noting that he did go back and get a GED and start a Stay in School campaign, he became very successful without a traditional education. Steve Jobs of Apple and Bill Gates of Microsoft never finished college. These two software giants are hardly considered failures. So being uneducated doesn't guarantee failure, and being educated doesn't guarantee success. If you truly want to maximize your potential, you need to challenge some of the deeply held beliefs and make sure they are not standing between you and the success you desire.

Dream

Through thought you can fantasize about anything. Let your imagination go. When we were kids we used to play "pretend" where we could live in any world we wanted and be whatever we wanted. The physical space where reality was set made absolutely no difference; I was able to be a superhero saving a princess from dragons or a bad guy or whatever went through my mind. My kids can get so involved in playing in their own world, I'll get yelled at when I walk into their room because I was stepping in a lake. Obviously there is no lake in the bedroom, but they certainly see it!

Several years ago, my wife and I took my then three-year-old niece to Chuck E. Cheese's. We were playing games and she was riding the motorized rides. At one point she asked us for a token to put into one of the motorized rocking horses. She put the money in and started watching the horse go back and forth. My wife and I clearly saw that nobody was riding the horse and thought she just didn't get on it before putting the money in and now wasn't sure how to get on it while it was moving. So, being a good uncle, I picked her up to get on the ride. She immediately fought me and started screaming "No! Dockey is on it!" Dockey was her imaginary friend at the time, but the fact that Dockey was just a figment of her imagination made absolutely no difference. Dockey was so real in her mind, her imagination worked so well, there was no convincing her that Dockey was not on the horse. So we watched the horse continue to rock back and forth, with no rider. After the ride ended I asked if Dockey enjoyed the ride, and for the record she did. For all intents and purposes in my niece's mind at that time, Dockey was real.

As we get older, we no longer allow our imagination to go wild. Our belief systems hold us back by some fictitious boundary called logic or reality. In our minds we find logical reasons that we cannot achieve something great. We might decide we don't like our lifestyle and that our income doesn't support the lifestyle we want. Your dream might be to have a vacation home at your favorite vacation destination. You want to fly there three or four times a year, and fly first class. You may want to live in a new luxury home in a prestigious location, where your kids can get a first-rate education. Then you look at your present salary and realize you will need to double, triple, or even improve your income by ten times what you make now. Wow, that is not logical—people don't just increase their income by a factor of ten. When this happens you tell yourself that the dream is not logical, you can't achieve it, and you won't even try. If you do decide to give it a shot, and you miss the mark on your first try, or don't see the results happening as fast as you'd like, then you'll retreat. You tried, it didn't work—I guess that lifestyle is meant for someone else.

To effectively dream, you need to first challenge those beliefs and start creating a vision and acting like your vision is real. You may come home to an old house that needs repair, but in your mind you should treat that house as your dream house. If you drive an old car that is well past its prime, treat that car as if it were the new car you desire so much. When you take your vacations, enjoy yourself as if you were already having your dream vacations. When you do this, you get emotionally involved in your dream, and this will change your belief system in your subconscious mind, and when your belief systems change you begin to allow yourself to chase bigger and better dreams.

There is a story about the painter Vincent van Gogh being asked how he was able to paint such wonderful pictures. Van Gogh responded, "I dream of a painting and then I paint my dream." This is easy to accomplish for a painting because on paper there are no rules or paradigms that prevent us from painting the dream. But what if you could dream of your ideal life and then live the dream? It is the same principle. When you dream of your ideal life and you create a fantasy reality in your mind so detailed and realistic and you hold that image in your mind to impress it, or burn it, into your subconscious mind, then your subconscious mind directs your body to act in a way that is consistent with realizing your dream.

Create the Vision

Once we have challenged our belief systems and really allowed ourselves to dream, the next step is to actually create the vision. For anyone to be successful, you need to have a life vision. You need to understand what you really want and have a plan for achieving it. You do this by picturing your idea of happiness. When you do this, it is perfectly acceptable to act like a five-year-old at Christmas: I want this lifestyle, I want this type of job, I want this car, I want this type of spouse, whatever you want. Your idea of happiness is your own personal paradise. Everyone has a different idea of paradise. Your dream house is different than mine; your dream job is different than mine.

So the question becomes what makes you happy? The answer to that question is your own personal life vision, and it comes from your dreams. Some people want to run companies; others want to be the best salesperson in the company or the best mechanic in the shop. What is important to me and what is important to you is not and will not be the same. If you think you want to be the CEO of a company, but the idea of the amount of work required in that job just makes you uncomfortable, then guess what, being a CEO is probably not really what you want to do. I had an engineer that worked for me and at one point he was toying with the idea of moving into management. When an opportunity came up, and I told him about it and he said he would think about it. Later I asked if he applied, and he said, "I thought about it but I really don't want a Blackberry. I'm happy where I am." He realized that management wasn't what he really wanted, so he and I worked on how he could maximize his potential with something that was in line with what his true desires were.

When you have an idea of what you want, visualize it. I mean really visualize it. Play pretend with your desires, with what you want. Pretend you have that job, car, or dream house. When you are playing pretend with whatever it is you want, you have to see it in your mind. Visualization is a common practice in sports, and oftentimes great players will visualize hitting a home run, scoring a goal, or hitting a free throw.

The book *Zen Golf* talks about visualizing your golf shot before even addressing the golf ball. When I golf, I will often try to describe the shot I want and I often say the words out loud. I am aiming for that tree, or I want to land short of that trap and roll it out to the middle of the fairway. The theory behind the visualization is if you can see the shot in your mind, your body can do it. To carry the golf analogy a little further you can "visualize the shot" in all aspects of life—it is the same principle. Visualize yourself getting up in your dream house, getting in your dream car, and going to your dream job, favorite fishing spot, favorite coffee shop. Visualize what makes you happy. Become so engulfed in your visions that you can feel the sensations you would feel if they were real. Describe your visions and say the words out loud so you can hear them.

This type of deliberate visualization is a tool used to call upon the law of attraction. The law of attraction says like attracts like, or in other words what you think about you bring about. The more you think about something and the more you visualize it, the faster the law of attraction works. I use this for every aspect of my life and for every project I take on. Visualization and the law of attraction alone do not solve the world's problems, but they are the first steps to success and happiness. In order to be successful or happy, you first need to be able to visualize what success and happiness look like.

It can be really easy to be a skeptic about this visualization technique and the law of attraction. *So if I picture something in my mind, I'll get it? Really? So if I picture $1 million I'll get it?* Yes, absolutely!

When I first read about the law of attraction in the books Robert recommended I admit I didn't fully understand how the law of attraction could actually be a law and as real as, say, the law of gravity, but I did keep an open mind. Robert is a successful man and he recommended these books; besides, if this is what worked for him there could be some truth in what I read.

I studied engineering in college, so therefore I have been trained that when I am presented with a theory, I cannot take it on faith alone and I look for some proof as to whether the theory is true. In this case I decided to find examples where others were successful and look to see if the theory worked.

Thomas Edison is the inventor of the incandescent light bulb. Early in his career Edison had a vision of electric lighting replacing the oil lamp as being the instrument that lights up the common household. Edison worked and worked to develop the incandescent light bulb and was met with failure after failure. Edison had unwavering determination to realize his dream. In actuality Edison failed thousands of times and is quoted as having said, "I have not failed. I've just found 10,000 ways that won't work." Edison had a belief and vision in his mind, the determination to realize his vision, and as a result today almost every house in America and the majority of the world has the ability to use electric lighting.

President John F. Kennedy entered the space race with a notable speech at Rice University on September 12, 1962, where he famously said, "We choose to go to the Moon in this decade and do the other things, not because they are easy, but because they are hard." President Kennedy had a vision of going to the moon and beating the Soviet Union in the space race. On July 20, 1969, the United States successfully landed a manned spacecraft, Apollo 11, on the moon and in "one small step for man, one giant leap for mankind" the United States defeated the Soviet Union in the space race. Even today, the United States is the only country to have ever put a man on the moon.

These are two stories of individuals that had a dream and a vision, and history is full of these types of stories—stories of a successful person with a vision and the dedication to accomplish that vision. Think of the Wright brothers with powered flight, or our country's founding fathers. Even the story about Petty Officer Swank achieving success in his Navy career, despite the challenges of not having any formal technical schooling and the expectations of others that he wouldn't be able to advance in his career is an example. These stories give me the evidence I should have needed to be unequivocally convinced that through the power of thought and faith I can accomplish anything.

To find a more relevant example, especially one that is closer to home I found my sister is an excellent example. In her senior year of high school she became pregnant and shortly afterward she had a little girl. As with all young single mothers this was a struggle for her. She needed to figure out what she was going to do after high school to find work and a place to live, just like all the rest of us at that age, but she also had someone else she was responsible for, and this someone was completely innocent and helpless as all infants and young children are. My sister had this belief that she was going to overcome her challenges and eventually have a successful career, get married, and raise a family. She met her goal and at the age of twenty-nine finished college with a psychology degree with a concentration in mental health; she has found a very successful career in sales, she married a man that I am proud to call my brother, and now she's raising the family she always wanted to raise. When she and I talked about this journey, she said there was never any doubt in her mind she was going to get what she wanted. She paid her dues; so to speak; she avoided the path of least resistance I spoke about earlier, she put in the work needed to achieve her goal, and most importantly she did not let her outside circumstances stop her from achieving her dreams.

However, it is human nature to believe that other people are able to accomplish things I am not capable of accomplishing, so I had to find examples in my own life where I had a vision and that vision materialized. The most vivid example in my mind was when I was in college; I wanted a Pontiac Grand Prix. I wanted it all decked out, with spoilers, dual exhaust, leather, and a moon roof. Every time I saw one drive by, I would say to myself and to whoever was with me that I wanted one. I told myself I was buying one as soon as I got a job after graduation. At one point, I remember being on a bus going on a field trip for an industrial engineering class to a washing machine factory. I was sitting toward the front of the bus and I could see out the front windshield. We were behind a Grand Prix, and I could see straight into the front seat and see the entire dashboard. I literally pictured myself in that seat driving that car. Sounds corny, right? Well, not long after that I was driving home from my part-time job and at a used car lot between my work and home, right there in front closest to the road was a white 2000 Pontiac Grand Prix GT coupe. I was compelled to stop and look it over. The price was in the right ballpark to make the payments within my reach with my part time job. While I was there I spoke to the sales guy, and I went off to see if I could secure financing because the dealer was clearly looking to make money on the loan that offered high interest rates with extended payment periods! Well, as it turned out my credit union had special financing at a low rate, but they wanted me to get a cosigner. I didn't have one, and because I don't like to ask others for money I didn't feel comfortable asking for one.

Later that week I was talking to my dad and told him about the car and I was trying to figure out how to get financing. He offered to cosign, which was somewhat of a shock. OK, maybe I dropped a hint about cosigning, but I didn't ask! In the end, I was able to negotiate a price I could live with and had financing in hand. I kept and drove that car for the next 10 years. Had I known the way visualization and the law of attraction would work, maybe I would have visualized driving a Ferrari!

In this story I had all the details down to the spoilers, dual exhaust, leather, and a moon roof. I pictured myself in the driver's seat. My visualizations were detailed and lifelike. I was picturing a pretty popular car at the time; therefore my visualizations were frequent because I would visualize myself in that car every time I saw one on the road or in a parking lot. No matter what you visualize, it has to be detailed, deliberate, and frequent.

Visualization takes place in the conscious mind. The conscious mind is where you can define what you want and where you actually see things in your mind. If I ask you to tell me what your house looks like, you would picture it in your conscious mind, describe it to me, and I would then picture it in my conscious mind.

When maximizing your potential, the act of visualization becomes the key action. Visualization has to be detailed, deliberate, and frequent. You have to find time daily or even several times a day where you can really focus and concentrate on the act of visualization. The more details you can provide to your visions, the stronger the impression will be on your subconscious mind.

Visualization works like magic, but your visions will not appear out of thin air. You are required to take positive action to realize your visions. Let us take the example of my desire to move into management. Nobody just gave me the job because I showed up to work. I had to take on tasks that gave me the opportunity to learn new skills and demonstrate the ability to lead and manage teams.

At times I had to work outside of my comfort zone. I worked late hours and furthered my education. This was a sacrifice of my free time and for my family. I did these things to attain my goal of becoming a manager. Through visualization I impressed upon my subconscious mind a desired outcome of my life, and through that I was able to recognize opportunities, and in some cases I actually created the opportunities needed for me to learn and grow in my position. Within a short time of constantly visualizing and taking action to realize my vision, a manager in my organization moved to another department. As she was leaving she recommended that I would be a good replacement for her previous position. As a result I was promoted into a management position.

Napoleon Hill, the author of *Think and Grow Rich*, writes in his book, "Whatever the mind can conceive and believe, the mind can achieve regardless of how many times you may have failed in the past or how lofty your aims and hopes may be." When this idea is put into practice, the transformational effects can and will bring about a level of successes that may have previously been thought to be unattainable. You can conceive of a lifestyle, a goal that you want to accomplish—that is the easy part. It is the belief system that needs to be challenged. But whenever you combine a dream with belief, you have to know that your dream will be achieved. I personally use this quote anytime the going gets tough and I need some inspiration.

I gave two examples of visualization working in my life: one of a material possession, the car, and another of a career goal, getting into management. In both instances I had a vision, and working through my subconscious mind I was able to develop the habits and recognize opportunities needed to attain my vision.

One important aspect to remember is that the subconscious mind does not pick up on negatives. Negative words simply do not register in the subconscious mind. If your goal is to become debt free, you cannot focus on becoming debt free. Even if in your conscious mind you are focusing on becoming debt free, the subject of your attention is on the debt. All that your subconscious mind understands is the debt. The secret to becoming debt free is to focus on living a wealthy lifestyle. In this scenario your mind picks up the wealthy part of the visualization and begins to form habits designed to attain that goal. Another quick example is don't visualize preventing illness, visualize being healthy. Visualize how you want your life to be, not how you don't want it to be.

Many people visualize being wealthy and living a life of abundance. There is nothing wrong with this, but your life of wealth and abundance can only be achieved and maintained if you attain your wealth through ethical means. I once sat in an ethics class that my company was giving. The woman they brought in to provide the ethics lectures repeated one point over and over, and it has stuck with me all these years: "The truth always finds a way to come to the surface." She provided example after example of people and companies trying to cover up unethical behavior. The truth always surfaced and the people responsible for the unethical actions were held accountable. As a result the success attained through unethical means was short lived and often resulted in losses greater than any success that was achieved.

An example of someone who tried to create success through unethical means was the con artist Bernie Madoff. Bernie Madoff would convince people to invest in his firm and would promise large returns that were really unattainable. This raised the concerns of a financial analyst named Harry Markopoulos. Harry went to the

SEC several times with evidence that the returns that Madoff was claiming were mathematically impossible. In the end it turned out that Madoff was operating a large Ponzi scheme worth billions of dollars. Although Madoff did achieve mass amounts of wealth and lived a life of abundance for a period of time, it all came crashing down in 2008 when the FBI arrested Madoff for securities fraud. Madoff was later convicted and sentenced to 150 years in prison. The truth will surface, and justice will prevail.

Habit

I have told some stories thus far in this book of some of my success, from being successful in my career adventures to being "one of those guys" while in the Navy. I clearly laid out that I do not believe anything was handed to me. So if things just don't come easy to me, what was the difference my shipmate was seeing between his performance and mine? Why did things appear to come easy for me while he struggled?

There are two reasons for this. First, I had developed a habit of being successful. While I was in the Navy I set a goal of being the most productive technician in the shop. I was confident that I would be able to accomplish this goal because in my previous work experience (although a completely different line of work) I had achieved high levels of success. The logical conclusion for me was that I was going to be successful wherever I was working. However, I didn't show up on the first day being the most productive member of the shop. I aligned myself with our technical representative, the expert if you will, to take on the more challenging problems. I would work with others in the shop that were experienced and knowledgeable about how our systems worked on the aircraft. I worked hard in

A-school (the Navy's technical school) and FRAMP School, where I became familiar with the aircraft I was assigned. I made it a goal to be successful, and made a habit of working hard to achieve the goal.

Habits are very strong instincts that humans develop. Ask anyone trying to change an undesirable habit, such as smoking, and listen to the struggles that person has when trying to quit. A daily routine is a habit. Every morning as I get ready for work, I do the same things, in the same order. I do these things without thinking. On occasion my wife or one of the kids will be up when I am getting ready for work and this will throw off my routine. When this happens, I am no longer operating in my subconscious, and it isn't uncommon in these circumstances for me to take longer getting ready or forget something and have to come back home for it. This is another example of the conscious and subconscious mind in action.

How do you develop a habit of success? You create a craving for success. How do you create a craving for success? You achieve success. Let us say your goal is to be healthier, and one of the things you have to do is become more active. Perhaps you will set a goal of running in a marathon. Many people set this goal to give them something to strive for when trying to get healthy. When you start out, depending on your level of fitness, you are not likely to go out and run a full 26.2 miles on day one. So you set smaller goals. This month I will run five miles, next month I will increase that to seven miles. As you achieve those goals take the time to celebrate your success. Feel good about getting that accomplishment. Soon, as you achieve more and more of your goals, and celebrate each one eventually your body (i.e., your subconscious mind will begin to crave that satisfaction). Once that craving begins, you have developed the habit of being successful. At this point the subconscious mind starts to help you recognize and take advantage of opportunities to help you satisfy that craving again and again and again. It is the same reflex or reaction that causes a smoker to crave another cigarette or an alcoholic to crave another drink, only not as destructive. In all these cases you've conditioned your mind to crave, and in some cases become addicted to, a certain stimulation, be it the rush of success or the chemical reaction caused by the nicotine of a cigarette.

Visualization and hard work are two of the secrets essential to achieving great personal success. If you visualize a goal, and are willing to put in the hard work to achieve the goal, I submit to you that anything is possible. No one person is greater than another, but when one person is willing to visualize a goal and has the determination to achieve the goal, that person will realize more success.

Having the Right Vision

For many years in my career I had a vision of leading engineering programs, probably moving into a profit and loss division. This seemed to be the right career path for me, as I had spent many years in school getting educated in engineering principles. Every day I took actions that would help me become a better technical leader. I progressed toward this goal with moderate success. Eventually, though, as I moved up the chain and the competition for positions became more challenging, I found myself in a plateau. Doors were no longer open for me, and when I would find an opportunity that I was interested in, I wasn't able to capitalize and get the position I desired. If and when I would have the opportunity to interview for a position on my presumed career path, I would somehow be unable to secure the position. I would be well qualified for the position, but I wasn't able to project that to the hiring managers. My career eventually felt stuck, and when this happened, like most people, I'd find excuses for why I wasn't getting promoted and it was never my fault.

This certainly was frustrating; however, after doing much studying, I eventually examined what I was doing and what role I was really playing in my sudden lack of career progression. I was already managing engineering programs and doing so successfully, so it wasn't a matter of qualifications. I started reflecting on where I derived my job satisfaction, and the answer was astonishing. I realized I derived absolutely no job satisfaction in the actual program management aspect of my job, yet program management jobs were where I was focusing my job search. Is there any wonder why I wouldn't interview well for these positions? Deep down I was pursuing the wrong vision—it wasn't in harmony with what I really enjoyed doing.

I then realized that my job satisfaction came from helping the people around me become more successful in their positions. Helping others realize their full potential, stretch and grow. I enjoyed coaching others to pursue their dreams and to better their lives. Once I did this, an entirely new set of doors opened and my career began to get traction again.

When you are working with something that is in line with your natural abilities it is easy to tell because you enjoy what you are doing. You want to go to work that day, and when you come home in the evening, you can't wait to get back to it the next day. When the end of the day comes, you cannot believe it is time to go home. In fact there are times when the time to go home was hours ago! As a junior engineer, I used to spend a lot of time in a lab. We would be testing products to make sure they do what is expected and make sure the products meet the requirements imposed on them. I can remember being the first one to arrive in the morning and last to leave in the evening. I was easily spending 12 to 13 hours a day in the lab and not running out of energy. I was doing what I truly enjoyed doing at that point in time. When the work you have to do totally consumes you and you lose track of time, then you truly can put in the work necessary to achieve your goals. This is a case of being in the zone, and when you are in the zone, time flies by.

Self-discipline and sacrifice are two other important attributes. In every example of where I was looked up to as successful or "one of *those* guys" I put in extra work to be viewed that way. Putting in the extra work, doing the extra studying, and taking on difficult tasks are a sacrifice. I had to sacrifice my free time and I had to put in extra effort. It would be much easier to sit and watch TV, but watching TV does not help me maximize my full potential. When you stop paying your dues, so to speak, you become complacent and plateau in your personal development.

Vision and the Mind

When you make a habit of deliberately creating a vision of something in your conscious mind, you are impressing that image in your subconscious mind. I had a firm image of me owning a Pontiac while I was in college. I thought about it every day, and as I previously described, all the actions fell in place to allow me to purchase that car. I believe this was all done because of the images I impressed upon my subconscious mind. I saw the car at the dealer that day and something inside me told me to pull over and look at it, and this something was the internal push originated in my subconscious mind. This is very much the same instinct that tells me to run when I see fire; it is the internal push that causes our bodies to take action.

When you visualize something and burn that image into your subconscious mind, your subconscious mind will work to make that visualization into a reality. The subconscious mind does not understand complexity, time, or money; it just eventually knows that your vision is something it must do. Just like the subconscious mind knows to run from fire and control your breathing, your subconscious mind will know how to recognize opportunities to fulfill the vision. This is the law of attraction I discussed earlier. Recall that the law of attraction says like attracts like, or in other words what you think about you bring about. This happens because your subconscious mind will recognize things your conscious mind may not, and your subconscious mind will lead you toward those things. Your subconscious mind is not dictated by paradigms. By visualizing your goal, whether it is hitting a golf ball, landing on the moon, or taking your business to the next level, your subconscious mind will work in the "zone" and give you the instinctive push to make decisions toward achieving your goals.

Now, your conscious mind has to go along, and this is where opportunities are often squandered. Your subconscious mind may identify an opportunity and the conscious mind may decide not to pursue the opportunity. Your conscious mind is where the risk reward trade study takes place. For example:

- I could open my own business, but what if I fail?
- I could ask her out on a date, but what if she says no?
- I could practice golf more, but it's a little chilly outside.

Your conscious mind creates the "buts." "Buts" are not always bad, and I am certainly not suggesting you ignore conscious thought;

conscious though is what separates humans form all other species. However, I am suggesting that you honestly evaluate the risks and rewards.

Let us reconsider the comments above:

- I could open my own business, but what if I fail? You fail. Worst case you get a job and try again. You obviously had a valuable skill and a job prior to opening your own business, and you could always do that again.
- I could ask her out on a date, but what if she says no? She says no, just a momentary embarrassment. What if she says yes?
- I could practice golf more, but it's a little chilly outside. My personal favorite, and have used this one often. Put on a sweatshirt or find a heated practice facility.

CHAPTER 4
Leadership

ONE ELEMENT NECESSARY to maximizing your potential is to be an effective leader. Truly successful people are people who have the ability to lead groups of other people toward a common goal. A team can always accomplish more than the individuals of that team could accomplish by working alone. The leader who can build a team that has the talent and skills needed to be successful will themselves be successful. Furthermore the leader must be able to direct this talent toward a common goal. Leaders of teams typically have higher earnings than the non-leaders on the team, precisely because of their ability to get groups of people to accomplish a common goal.

Most of us have worked with someone we really liked. It could be a boss, a religious leader, community leader, or a sports coach.

I have probably been personally influenced by someone in all these areas. There are people that if I ever have the chance to work for again, I will. There are also others that I will avoid. I have met religious leaders who have convinced me to return to the church, and others who made me feel like attending church was a waste of my time. In high school I had a basketball coach who invested his time in me to help me become a better basketball player. I wrote about my lead petty officer when I was in the Navy, and how I left a company because my boss didn't seem to care.

We all know that leadership is a frequently discussed topic at many companies, and it is almost always talked about in the context of a characteristic desired in management. It is identified in people at the lower levels of the hierarchy, and these people are groomed for upper management. The question is how do you identify leadership qualities, and how do you grow them? What is a leader? Is it someone who is an expert in their field? Maybe. Is it someone who can get a job done? Maybe. Is it someone who people admire? Maybe.

The answer is quite simple: a leader is a person whom one or more people follow. You cannot be a leader if there are not people following you. So the definition of a leader is very broad. Every company and organization that has a hierarchical structure has leaders; there are just good leaders and bad leaders. Your boss is a leader; the president of the United States is a leader. CEOs of companies are leaders. In addition to people being leaders based on their position in some hierarchical structure, a leader can be someone who is able to inspire others around them and rally them to a cause. For example, when watching sports, you will hear announcers often talk about the leadership demonstrated by this player or that player. The players are not the coach, so they are not in any real management position, but they do inspire those around them and get them to rally toward a common cause. So then the question becomes what makes a good leader, and why do we care?

Let us start with why we care. Good leaders will fundamentally change organizations and usually for the better. Let us start with the premise that a good leader is a person other people want to follow. I am sure we can all relate to a boss or a person of authority that we did not agree with and couldn't wait until that person wasn't in that position any more. Good leaders will raise the passion and enthusiasm of the people they lead. Enthusiasm and passion create energy. Any engineer or scientist will tell you that energy is the substance that gets work done. Without energy, nothing can happen—period.

When a leader is creating energy, productivity will necessarily and proportionally increase. The more energy, the more work can get done. People who are energetic are more creative, motivated, and determined to complete a job or task right. They take pride in their work and are more willing to help those around them. Companies like Gallup sell services where they survey the people at companies to determine how engaged employees are. Gallup is really measuring the effectiveness of a company's leaders. Gallup has developed 12 questions geared to measuring the energy, enthusiasm, and effectiveness of the teams in their organizations. The reason companies pay Gallup for this service is because engaged employees are more productive. What leader doesn't want to improve productivity without increasing manpower or capital investments? As a leader myself, I realize that if I want to maximize the productivity of my team, I just have to create that energy—it's just that simple.

If we want to be great leaders what do we need to do? Have people want to follow you.

Be Inspirational

If a leader is someone that other people want to follow, then that leader must inspire others to follow them. A huge factor in inspiring others is the ability to clearly articulate your vision of where the team should go. People are unlikely to follow a leader who doesn't have a clear vision of where they are trying to go. Another aspect that helps inspire others is the ability to project an air of confidence. Projecting confidence should not be confused with arrogance. Arrogance is akin to entitlement or elitism, which is not a desirable quality. People don't willingly follow arrogance for an extended amount of time. Arrogant people tend to treat others as inferior, and feeling inferior does not inspire and therefore is counterproductive to maximize the human potential.

General George S. Patton could be described as an arrogant man. Patton was not well liked among his peers; he was loud and felt superior to his peers. For example, when invading Italy during World War II, Patton was asked to fight alongside his English counterpart General Montgomery, but he deliberately disobeyed orders in an attempt to beat Montgomery to the objective with the intention of gaining the glory. Patton was successful, but it is this type of grandstanding that is evidence of his arrogance and a reason for his peers' disdain. You could make the argument that Patton was a successful general—after all, achieving the rank of a four-star general is quite an accomplishment. However because of Patton's arrogance he was removed from command of the 3rd Army, and as a result Patton was not part of the Normandy invasion on D-Day. Patton was intentionally left out because of his arrogance and his treatment of those in his command. Early in the war General Omar Bradley was an officer reporting to General Patton. General

Bradley was known as a soldier's leader, meaning that he could relate to the men over whom he had command. The difference in leadership styles allowed Omar Bradley to be promoted through the ranks and by the end of the war he was Patton's superior officer.

Confidence, on the other hand, gives people a sense that you are comfortable with where you are going and your ability to get there. Confidence comes from the faith that you can and will accomplish your objective and that your vision will provide people with a better future than they have today.

Be Humble

I had a boss tell me one time that in his younger years he was arrogant. He was smart, and he knew what he was doing, but his career was becoming stagnant. He told me that it was not until his wife pointed out his flaw, in not so polite terms, that he even realized it. A humble leader knows when to ask for help and knows where his blind spots are. Not everyone can know everything; we all need help. Without the humility to acknowledge the blind spots and where they need help, a leader cannot be successful. One thing that makes a team successful is for each member to be able to complement their teammates' skills. A company needs someone who can do the bookkeeping, someone who can run the IT department, someone in sales, and someone who can understand the technical needs to upgrade a manufacturing floor. It takes all kinds of skills, and a leader needs to know where their unique skills are so they can get the help needed.

Leaders are human, just like the rest of us. Humans are flawed and make mistakes. A leader has to be humble enough to admit their mistakes and make a course correction when necessary. You may have a vision for a destination and a plan to get there. What happens if your plan isn't getting you there? You can blindly drive down the same road, hoping the road will get back on course, but hope is not a plan. A leader has to be able to recognize when a course correction is necessary and have the humility to say, this is not the right path, we need to refocus over here.

Many times, during my development as a leader, I've tried things that haven't worked out. I have worked on several different approaches for delivering bad news or articulating my vision. Some have worked, others haven't. When they do not work, I just try it again with a different approach.

Be Yourself

The best way to have people want to follow you is to be yourself. Nobody likes a phony. When you ask people on the street if they trust politicians, the answer is generally no. Why? Because politicians have a reputation of saying whatever needs to be said to get elected. You have to be true to yourself and you have to be genuine and authentic. If people do not believe you are genuine and authentic, then people will not choose follow you.

I am generally an introverted person and somewhat analytical in nature. I collect information, process it, digest it, and really have to let it sink in. It sometimes seems like a slow process that will frustrate me, but it is just the way I am. I am aware of this, and oftentimes when I take on a new role or challenge, I am very quiet at first and probably appear disinterested or disengaged. I just don't always feel I have much to add, and I typically need to digest information before I can even formulate questions and opinions. As I said, this frustrates me, and I am always self-conscious about it.

Typically when I take on a new role I will advise the people I am working with, the people that asked for my help, of how I work. While having these conversations, I let everyone know that I am not disinterested or disengaged. I have found that typically I am overly self-conscious, and my concerns are unwarranted, and in the end I am able to contribute and be productive and everyone benefits.

I have to live within my natural tendencies and be true to who I am. I cannot fake being something I am not and force myself into situations before I am fully ready to contribute. Imagine the disaster that would happen if I were to force myself to behave in a manner that is inconsistent with my natural tendencies? If I were to jump in and start making decisions without going through my natural process of collecting and analyzing information, I would likely make decisions that were ill-informed, not well thought out, or that I would have to reverse at a later date. If I acted in this manner I would certainly lose any credibility and would not be asked to help on future projects. It would be a career killer. On the other hand, by accepting my natural tendencies and going through my process, I am able to add value to the projects I am asked to support and everyone wins.

Be Accessible

Leaders need to be available to their teams at all times. For example, in my experience working on the space shuttle program, my manager was not aware of what I was doing. He was blind to the work I was doing and the work most of his team was doing. He wasn't accessible, and even when he would ask us what we were working on in our staff meetings, it appeared he wasn't interested. I made a commitment at that time, that when I grew into a position of leadership, I would be accessible to my team.

We all hear our management tell us that they have an open-door policy, but most of us really do not want to bother the boss. We think the boss probably has more important things to do than to hear our problems. At least that is how the thought process goes for most of us. Typically if I need something from my boss, unless I see him or her on a daily basis I am inclined to wait until the next staff meeting to bring it up. So it could be a week before I say something, and if the staff meeting is cancelled it might be two weeks. Now, of course if something is urgent, I may call or send an email, but typically I would bring less urgent issues up at a staff meeting.

So I know that is how I approach my boss; therefore I have to assume that my direct (and even indirect) reports approach me the same way. No matter how many times I say I have an open door policy, I have to imagine that it is not being taken advantage of like it could be. I know this because people tell me new information at my staff meetings, so I know they were waiting for that opportunity to bring it up.

The key is to make yourself available and accessible. I employed the concept of "management by walking around" (MBWA). I would engage my direct and indirect reports in the hallway or at their workspace. This showed that their work was important to me, because I didn't make them come to me. I am not above them in some artificial way, and I respect them. I found this to be an extremely useful tool to make myself accessible to those who reported to me.

When I discovered the MBWA technique I could not believe how powerful this tool really was. I was always good at walking around and checking in with my direct reports, but I never really made an attempt to talk to indirect reports—until I took on a new job at a new campus where I didn't know anyone and I had to find ways to interact with different people. Walking around the office and seeing those I was working with in their offices, cubes, and labs had a positive effect on team morale. Eventually the boss wasn't someone that stayed in their big office and summoned subordinates when desired. I saw who they were, commented on their pictures or their favorite sports teams. I got to hear about families, home projects, and hobbies. All this and we still talked shop. Getting to know my team on a personal level was as simple as stopping by a few times a week to say "hi." That simple interaction allowed them to naturally open up. I always asked how things were going and I would eventually hear the unfiltered truth, which is the most valuable information for managing teams and projects. I would be told what is going well, where there were struggles, the conflicts my team members may have, and requests for help when it was needed instead of just waiting for the next staff meeting. It was amazing. It was then my job to take action where they needed help and just let them vent when venting was appropriate. I did this with both direct and indirect reports.

MBWA does take time, and the larger the team, the more time it takes, but in reality the investment pays off. If you are able to find out about problems early, you can address them early, and usually in time for a reasonable and cost-effective solution to be implemented. And an unintended byproduct is you get to make a few new friends along the way. When you, as the boss, need something from your reports, they will be much more likely to pitch in and help out if you have a personal relationship with them. It is the most effective way I have found to create the atmosphere of shared results.

You can lead a horse to water but you can't make him drink. You can go to someone's workspace but you can't make them talk. What

I mean is, just because I showed up to talk to someone didn't mean that they were going to automatically tell me what was going on. Comfort grows with familiarity. So I learned over time that just the act of showing up, and perhaps just engaging in some small talk, would open the team up, so when there were problems or a team member needed help, they would be more comfortable discussing it with me. No policy can force someone to trust you, but there are simple rules of society and human nature that can be employed to build that trust.

Time Management

The funny thing about time is we all have the same amount: we all have only 24 hours in a day. We often hear people say that they don't have time to do this, or they'd like to do that but they don't have time. I want to get better at playing golf, but I don't have time to spend hours at the driving range to practice. However, there are people who are extremely successful and take on multiple challenges at the same time. There are many successful people who run businesses, write books, and donate time to help others. We all have the same 24-hour day, so how do others seem to get so much done? The secret isn't time management but managing what you do with your time.

In the book *The Science of Getting Rich* Wallace D. Wattles states, "Every day is either a successful day or a failure. And, it is the successful days which get you what you want." Wattles then goes on to say, "Do, every day, all that can be done that day." One of the lessons learned is you cannot go back and do yesterday's work today, nor can you go into the future and do the work of tomorrow. However, you can focus on the work that needs to be done today and execute today's work successfully.

There are many techniques used for managing time, and several books have been written on the subject of time management. I will admit that it is hard to make managing your time a habit; however, when I am in the habit of managing my time properly my effectiveness dramatically improves. If you make a list of the most important things you must do each day to achieve your goals and complete those tasks in a successful manner, then you have been successful. Do not make your list so extensive that you cannot complete all the tasks, or you are unable to enjoy your life. Your list should be short enough to deal with the issues of the day. I know in my job there are often times that people come to me to help them deal with a problem or to make a decision on one thing or another. This is part of my job and is important to deal with.

This is not a daily shopping list of things to do like pick up the kids from practice, go to the dry cleaners, and pick up dinner on the way home. This list should include tasks and activities specifically tailored to achieving your goal. Some things I put on my daily list are:

- show gratitude by thanking someone for their help
- actively mentor someone
- spend time to study something important to achieving my goals
- learn something that will help me be more effective at work.

Creating the list is important because it forces you to think about the actions you need to do to be successful and what actions you might be taking that are counterproductive or hinder your progress toward your goals. In addition to using your list to manage your time effectively, at the end of the day when you check off the items from your list, you will feel a sense of accomplishment, and that will start to create the craving for more successful days. If you are successful each day, you will be successful in life.

CHAPTER 5
Attitude

ATTITUDE IS DEFINED as a settled way of thinking or feeling about someone or something, typically one that is reflected in a person's behavior. Because a person's attitude is reflected in their behavior, it is sometimes easy to intuitively know what a person is thinking or feeling about a certain thing. I had a time when I felt I was being mistreated by my superior officers while I was in the Navy, which resulted in me being actively disengaged. To any observer it was obvious I was thinking and feeling mistreated, and my behavior and attitude reflected that. At work, I have seen people struggling with a project or problem, and when it gets somewhat overwhelming, you can see the physical effects of that, such as slumped shoulders and irritability. On the other hand, when people have things going their way, so to speak, they seem to have a little pep in their step; they smile more and are generally more jovial.

I have elementary-school-age kids and most days when I get home from school, my wife and kids are at the kitchen table doing homework. Unfortunately my kids don't find the inherent pleasure in learning at this time and they do not want to be doing homework, and their behaviors reflect that. They have a bad attitude and are more irritable, less receptive to help when they make mistakes, and are often picking fights with each other and their mother. I guess misery loves company. Sometimes I am able to turn around the atmosphere, just by taking a fresh approach and because I just got home they are not mad at me yet. However, most of the time that doesn't work. When they are showing a bad attitude and affecting other people's attitudes, I often tell them they have to fix their attitude and fix it now.

Because I often told my kids they needed to fix their attitudes, and it rarely resulted in them changing their attitude, I wasn't sure if my kids knew what their attitude actually is and what it means when I say to fix their attitude. When I asked them what it means, they described it as their feelings: a bad attitude was when they were feeling bad, and to fix it they need to start feeling good. When I tell them to fix their attitude I want them to get in a better state of mind, where they can be happy, productive, energetic, and pleasant to be around. On the occasions when they do have good attitudes, the homework gets done faster, and they find that they have time to do things they enjoy like watch TV or play games. The other benefit of them having good attitudes is that my wife and I are more likely to allow snacks or treats after dinner.

Monday Morning

Not many people like Mondays. I don't know how many times on a Monday morning at work I would say good morning, or how are you, something like that, and the response would be a begrudging "It's Monday" or "Is it Friday yet?" With just a little research on the Internet you will find article after article on "Sunday Night Stress Syndrome" or "Sunday Night Blues." This stress occurs to many people and causes restlessness and anxiety about the thought of going to work the following morning. I admit at points in my life I would feel some anxiety on Sunday evening and would have trouble sleeping. In my opinion if someone is dealing with a particularly difficult issue at work, I understand the anxiety, but it shouldn't be a constant strain.

What if you could look at Monday mornings with excitement and enthusiasm? Imagine looking forward to starting your week. Can you imagine how much more energy you would have and how much more productive you could be? It is just a shift in attitude, where Monday mornings can be considered your favorite time of the week, which actually impacts your Sunday evening. Most people make New Year's resolutions, because a new year is a fresh start of sorts. Others might make a similar resolution for their birthday. These are certainly good things to do, but why wait for an annual anniversary to make a difference? Look at Monday mornings as a fresh start, and the advantage is Mondays are more frequent than a new year. You can look back at the previous week and evaluate what can be done differently in the upcoming week to be a better person, employee, leader, spouse, parent, etc., and make a decision to do something differently. Enter each week full of optimism, with a list of things you can accomplish that week. When you look back at the end of the week, you can see all the things you accomplished and feel a real sense of accomplishment. If there are items on your list you were unable to complete, don't let that depress you, just add those unaccomplished tasks to your list for next week.

When you start this, people may look at you like you're crazy or, more often than not, will think you are joking on Monday mornings when you say, "It's Monday morning, my favorite time of the week." Think about it: which attitude would you prefer to start your week with, the attitude where you are dreading the next five days or the attitude where you look forward to the upcoming week with optimism and enthusiasm? Either way, you have the full week in front of you and your attitude toward it will make a tremendous difference in the results.

Responding versus Reacting

When events happen to us in our lives we can either react to them or respond, and there is a significant difference. A reaction is typically a "knee-jerk" action that just happens. For example, if you scream at me, I might react by screaming back. If you hit me, I may react by hitting you back. Normally reacting is not the best course of action. However if you learn to respond to a situation instead of reacting, your actions will be completely different. For example, if you scream at me, I could respond calmly and be level headed. If you hit me I can respond by walking away. A response is the result of composed thinking, which typically is a response to training and repetition.

When I played sports as a child, I was taught to respond to certain situations with a specific behavior. As a quarterback, I would respond to defensive pressure by stepping up in the pocket to avoid a sack. As a basketball player I would respond to a defensive player with a specific action to get a teammate or myself free from the defender. In baseball when a ball was hit I would respond with the appropriate defensive play. As an adult I coach my children with their sports, and I can tell you with all certainty that when a kid reacts to a baseball being hit, they will rarely be in the proper position to make a good defensive play. They need to be taught how to respond when a baseball is hit and where to go to make a play.

Members of the military and first responders constantly drill, which is another word for practicing or rehearsing. They rehearse specific maneuvers, crisis situations, and battle-specific scenarios. These drills can be fairly elaborate and complex, but the entire purpose is for our military and first responders to respond in a crisis instead of reacting. They train this way, so when they are faced with a real-life scenario, they respond appropriately and effectively. If they were to just react, there would be chaos, which would inevitably result in tragedy.

A good example of responding versus reacting happened on January 15, 2009. On that day most of the news coverage was dominated by what will be referred to as the "miracle on the Hudson." This was when a US Airways flight was departing New York City's LaGuardia Airport and ran into several birds, which resulted in both engines of the Airbus A320 failing. The pilot, Captain Chesley B. "Sully" Sullenberger, and First Officer Jeffrey Skiles realized they would not be able to navigate the aircraft to a nearby airfield and made the quick decision to land the aircraft in the Hudson River. Because of the aircrew's ability to respond to the crisis, all passengers and crew were safely recovered from what could have very easily been a tragic event.

They way to ensure that you respond instead of reacting in any given situation is to maintain control over your emotions. During any type of disaster, such as a storm or a fire, the first thing you'll hear from the first responders is to not panic. When people panic, they react and chaos ensues and inevitably the damage caused by the catastrophe is escalated by the resulting panicking.

In February of 2003, the rock band Great White was performing in a club in Rhode Island and the band was using some pyrotechnics during the show. The venue wasn't properly equipped for the pyrotechnics and the entire club quickly burst into flames. The majority of the patrons panicked, and their reaction was to run for the door where they entered. There was a stampede, and people were literally stuck in the doorway with no way to get out. Some people responded and found an alternative exit and were able to escape the fire; unfortunately many of those who reacted did not escape and 100 people were killed by the fire. This is an example that demonstrates that those people who responded when they saw the fire were able to escape, while a large number of those who reacted ended up dying.

To respond rather than react you need to maintain control over your emotions. You don't have to be responding to a dual engine failure or a fire at a nightclub to realize the benefits of responding over reacting. In the workplace sometimes tempers can get heated or something on your project doesn't go as planned, and it is what you can do next that will make the difference. When a colleague gets upset and starts raising their voice you can decide what actions you will take—you will decide whether you will respond or react. It is advisable to maintain control over your emotions and project an attitude of confidence and calmness. First of all, this will quickly defuse any tension, because when emotions are running hot people are less receptive to hearing other people's opinions and become defensive. I have actually seen people being defensive and argue about something when they both had the same opinion. They didn't recognize it because they were defensive and not listening. What a complete waste of time and energy it is to argue with someone when there is no difference of opinion. Maintaining control over your emotions allows dialog, calculated actions, and avoids undesired results.

How will you respond when life happens? Some people panic, others freeze, and others lead. You can prepare yourself for various situations through the power of visualization. This is what Dr. Denis Waitley meant when he said, "If you go there in the mind, you will go there in the body." Visualizing certain situations before you are presented with them helps you recognize the desired course of action when a situation presents itself. It is extremely helpful to visualize an interview before you go into the interview. Run through "what if" scenarios for situations that you might be faced with. When I coach my son's baseball team, at practice we simulate game time situations. I'll ask the players what they do if the ball is hit to them in a given situation. I want them thinking about it before the ball is hit so the decision of what to do is predetermined and they can respond instead of reacting.

Another example of a predetermined decision would be if a person is on a diet or doesn't drink alcohol. When that person is offered a piece of cake or an adult beverage, they don't have to think about their response: the decision has already been made. Visualizing situations can help you be prepared for what life throws at you, and when situations present themselves you will respond instead of react. It is that attitude and confidence that will give you control over the events in your life instead of the events having control over you.

Luck

I have had several conversations in my life where I was talking to a friend about successful people, and there always seems to be an element of luck. One simple example: my great-grandfather invested wisely in the stock market and was able to get in on some big companies like Coke, Disney, and Black and Decker before they were big. He made good money off these investments as well as other investments. I remember hearing this as a kid, thinking, wow, that was lucky. But was it luck? I don't have the opportunity to talk to my great-grandfather, but I would be shocked if he said he was lucky. He did the homework and research necessary to develop a strategy that enabled him to be able to pick stocks that were most likely to provide a healthy return on his investment. He didn't just wake up one morning and say, "I want to invest in Disney, let's see how this goes."

Throughout my life when I wanted something, or wanted to experience something, I put in my mind what I wanted through visualization. From there I would focus on it as part of my daily routine. I would make a habit of visualization. When I did that, I impressed upon my subconscious mind what I wanted. My subconscious mind drives my instincts—that gut feeling that tells us what we should and should not do. My subconscious mind would drive me to make the decisions, recognize the opportunities, and take advantage of them, so that when I am in the right place at the right time I am able to recognize and capitalize on it. Simply stated, everyone creates their own luck, either good or bad, based on the thoughts they repeat over and over.

On the other hand, if you are continuously thinking about things you don't want, your subconscious mind will drive you to those opportunities as well. If you have ever said to yourself, "Why does this always happen to me?" it is because you are continuously thinking about being a victim to whatever keeps happening, and your subconscious mind attracts that action. For example, on my regular golf course I have a lot of confidence in myself on the first hole. It's a short par 4, and most of the time I can start my round with a par or the occasional birdie (one under par). Now, I'm not a great golfer, so pars are rare and a birdie only happens a few times a year. So I am usually feeling good about how I started my round until I get to the second hole, where I have much less confidence. The hole is set up with woods to the right, but far enough right that I can still miss-hit the ball and land safely. However, I almost always hit a big slice, causing the ball to curve the deep into the woods. On occasion I do manage to hit a long straight shot, which is desired, but the ball will still land in the woods. When that happens my playing partner will immediately say I was aimed that way. What? Really? Why did I do that? I believe this is because in my subconscious mind I am thinking about those woods, and now every time I play that hole I hit the ball into those woods. I am saying to myself, *Don't hit it in the woods*, but my subconscious mind is focused on the woods. What I need to do is change my thought pattern before I get to the second hole, so I am as confident as I am on the first hole. I need to create my own luck.

Anyone can create their own luck, simply by focusing on what you want, impressing it upon your subconscious mind, and from there letting nature take its course. It is really an amazing and powerful concept when you fully understand the power of it and are able to put this into action.

Positive Thinking

Charles R. Swindoll is credited with the quote "Life is 10% what happens to you and 90% how you react to it." There are so many things that happen in life that you cannot control. You cannot fully control how other people will act, you cannot control the weather, you cannot control the economy, and the list can go on and on. Unfortunately, each of these things impacts your life on a daily basis. Your spouse might do or say something you don't like. Gas prices can go up, making it more expensive to get to work, or even buy a gallon of milk for the kids. Your house can be destroyed by a hurricane, flood, or tornado. You have no control of these things. However, you do have to deal with them when they happen. It is how you deal with them that matters. I can go into example after example of where I have seen something unfortunate happen to someone, and they react negatively to it and their life spirals out of control. On the other hand, I've seen people use things like a divorce or the loss of a job and turn it into a new start and prosper.

Many times positive thinking really is just recognizing the silver lining in the clouds. At one of my previous assignments, I was known to have a positive and optimistic attitude. At times this was completely out of sync with the people I was working with. My colleagues and team members would run down a list of bad things that had happened on the program, and when something did go right, they were just waiting for the bad to happen next. When I joined that program, I will say the outlook was not very positive. Things were going poorly, and every day it seemed we were hit with another issue we had to resolve. It was hard to keep up with everything, let alone stay positive with the barrage of bad news that kept coming. However, within a year, we completely turned things around, and in my opinion we were able to turn the negative perceptions of the team members and management around. On occasion, even after the successes, we would still run into challenges, and I would hear, "Oh here we go again." And I would say, yes, once again we have the opportunity to prove how valuable we are, and how we can be successful!

Positive thinking doesn't mean that you can go through life thinking the glass is half full and will always remain that way. I said that I have a reputation of being positive, and I am. I am positive that with the right planning, leadership, and appropriate action my teams will be successful. I have a positive attitude because I have built a habit of success. I have confidence in my abilities, because every time I am put to the test I have succeeded.

Positive thinking alone will not necessarily lead to positive results. If what you do is truly just positive thinking, it is just thought and stays in your conscious mind. However, when you mix positive thinking with positive emotions, that leads to a positive attitude, and a positive attitude drives passion, and passion creates energy.

Passion

We have all heard the expression, "If you do something you love you'll never work a day in your life." In other words, if you are passionate about something you will have no problem spending your energy on it. Passion is the measure of how badly you want something. It is a thermometer of your desire. Being really passionate about something indicates you really want something. Being nonchalant about something indicates you probably can do without it. Pursue your goals that you are passionate about. Nobody becomes great at something that they do not feel passionate about.

Using the thermometer as an analogy is very appropriate: when passion runs hot it creates energy. If you are doing something you are passionate about you will feel as though you have never-ending energy, and after spending a day on it you will wonder where the time went. Personally I can spend an entire day playing golf and be at the golf course for five to six hours, and when it is all over I wonder how time went by so fast. I am passionate about playing golf. Passion is important because passion drives energy and energy is the force that is needed to accomplish work.

Passion is an emotion, and when you mix emotion and determination toward accomplishing something it gives that something energy. The combination of emotion and determination is the force that creates physical objects from ideas. For example, Edison was determined to develop the electric light bulb; he had the passion to pursue his goal, and today everyone in America and most of the civilized world has the ability to light their homes using electricity.

This is a powerful concept because it means that anything can be accomplished with the mere combination of determination and passion. This combination, however, has to be directed toward a positive end. Let us say that you were very passionate about ending poverty. Now this is certainly a noble goal, but your passion would be misguided. A goal of ending poverty would require focusing and spending energy on ending poverty, which is the problem. The subtleties of the English language do not register with the subconscious mind. The subconscious mind doesn't focus on ending poverty, it just focuses on the poverty. So passionately pursuing ending poverty will have a counter-effect.

Many of us want to change some outcome we don't particularly like. For example, you may not have much satisfaction in your current profession. When this happens it is common to focus on all the aspects of your job that cause you to be unsatisfied. When you focus on what you don't want, what actually happens is you attract or cause more of the same results. One way to look at this is by recognizing that everything has an opposite. The opposite of poverty is abundance and the opposite of success is failure. When you find that you are being overwhelmed with a circumstance or a condition that you find displeasing, an effective strategy is to look at the opposite. One tactic I use when coaching people that aren't particularly satisfied with their work is to ask them to describe their favorite part of their job. By focusing on the aspects of their jobs they do like oftentimes they will change their perspective on their job. It is natural for us to focus on what we do not like, but when we are in this situation, we can quickly and easily change that perception by listing and focusing on what it is we do like. Then the next step is to create a plan that will allow us to do more of what we enjoy doing and less of what we do not enjoy. It is rare that someone will like all aspects of their job, but by focusing on the aspects you do like, you can regain that passion for your career and reconnect with what got you started in that career path.

CHAPTER 6
Building a Team

HAVING A VISION, creating goals, and a plan to execute is an important part of maximizing the human potential, whether it is for the attainment of a personal or a professional goal. However, the best plan cannot be executed if there isn't anyone there to execute it, and you will be so much more effective and efficient when you have a team of people supporting you. If your goal is large, and it requires you going after something you've never done before (and it should) you will not know everything you need to know to attain your goal. No one person can know everything about everything, it would simply take too much time for one person to gather and master all that information for themselves, so to accomplish any big goal you will need the resources of other people, and this is your team.

When every member of your team is successful doing what is expected of them, the team will be successful. As a leader, it is your job to ensure that the people you are leading are successful in their work. This does not mean that the people you lead are not to be challenged, they absolutely should be challenged. This is how they will learn, grow, and advance in their work and become more productive and increase their own value. However, as a leader you need to make sure that when people are challenged you provide the resources needed to allow the person to produce a successful outcome. This may mean mentoring or providing the training necessary for your team members to be successful.

Equally important is to show your commitment to your team and really being available to help them when they do need help. We already discussed MBWA, which is a useful technique. However if you know that there are certain members of your team who have taken on an assignment that has taken them out of their comfort zone, it is important that you (the leader) set aside an appropriate amount of time to check in, coach, and mentor someone until the discomfort subsides. This clearly doesn't mean you do the work for them, but it does send the message to your team that you are committed to seeing them be successful and when someone takes on a challenge that takes them out of their comfort zone, they do not feel that they are left alone.

Leaders absolutely want to have their team members be willing to take on challenges that will make them uncomfortable. This is where real growth happens. In order for people to overcome the fear that is caused by being uncomfortable, they need to understand that they will have help getting to where they need to go. If someone is pushed outside their comfort zone without any support, they will be unlikely to accept the challenge. Additionally it will be harder for you to challenge others to step outside their comfort zone as well.

Identify Talent

When you've defined your vision and your goal, you will need to identify what skills and resources are needed for you to attain your goal. You will need to build your team to accomplish your goal, whether it is to accomplish an assignment at work, or to help with a personal goal. Usually identifying the skills is pretty simple, if you had a personal goal of exercising more to get in better health, your team may consist of your doctor and maybe a personal trainer. If you were working on a project at work, you may identify the disciplines you need for that task. However, getting the right people on the team is as important, and maybe more important than the actual skills the people possess. Successful people tend to surround themselves with successful people. This is no accident; they do this because success breeds success. On the other hand, if you surround yourself is mediocrity, you will achieve mediocrity.

As a football fan, in the 1990s and early 2000s Bill Cowher of the Pittsburgh Steelers would draft talented players every year. Cowher and the Steelers would draft the best athletes available who demonstrated great potential and not necessarily draft to fill a specific position—at least that is how I interpreted it. Some examples of talented athletes that Cowher drafted were Kordell Stewart and Antwaan Randle El, both fine gifted athletes able to fill a multitude of roles on the team, as well as Troy Polamalu, who was one of the most exciting strong safeties in the league. When I watched these players I realized that drafting for talent was an effective way to recruit. Coach Cowher would get the talent and then he would find where he could use them to be successful. The Steelers had a 62.3% win percentage, eight division championships, and two Super Bowl appearances with one Super Bowl win during Coach Cowher's successful 15-year career. Coach Cowher accomplished this because he would pick up the best talent that was available and groom them for success. Coach Cowher knew that with the right talent, he could build a successful team.

Develop Talent

As leaders and managers we need to be continuously looking for opportunities to increase the effectiveness of our team—in other words our teams need to continuously be improving. If we are not developing the talent of our team members, we are failing our team members. Team members that are not growing and moving forward in their careers are not contributing to their maximum potential. Many times, these people will consider themselves subject-matter experts (SMEs) in their particular job and they take this as a license to coast on what they know, and oftentimes rely on past successes as evidence that they are significant. I am not saying that SMEs are not a valuable part of any and all organizations—they most certainly are valuable. We need experts in engineering, accounting, marketing, sales, etc. Teams can't achieve their maximum potential without competent people to execute strategy and projects. The danger is when the individuals become complacent and believe they no longer see a need to perfect or sharpen their skills. These individuals are content being an expert rather than striving to be the expert that others experts strive to become. There is always something to learn in every field, no matter how much you already know.

People will follow those who make them better. The best leaders are the best teachers and the best teachers are the best leaders. Part of the job of being a great leader is to teach, guide, and coach those who work with you. Leaders allow individuals to sometimes fail, because just like taking risks is important to your development, learning to fail and learn from setbacks is important for you to help your team grow and succeed. When someone struggles and perhaps fails, it is your job as a leader to provide the coaching and guidance to help that person learn from their mistakes so they can grow as a person. Encourage that person to continue to take risks and challenge them to continue to push their comfort zone. In reality nobody fails until they quit.

Leaders need to lead by example in this respect. You may fail or struggle in front of your team; you are human and it is going to happen. Teamwork is a two-way street: when you are struggling, ask your team for help. Explain the situation and allow them to offer support and advice. This may seem counterintuitive, but the leader doesn't have to know all the answers, and by asking for help you will actually bolster the relationship you have with your team. It is important that your team looks at you as the leader of the team, not a person that is above the team. You expect them to rely on each other for support and to rely on you for guidance. In return you should rely on them for support when needed.

When you fail, and at some point you will, let it be a lesson on how to be successful the next time. Let your team see that you learned from your mistakes and that you are able to move on and not quit, because quitting is the real failure. Leadership is about coaching and mentoring. Giving back is the most important part of leadership.

Mentoring

Mentoring is an important part of developing talent, and I can say without any uncertainty I would not have had the successes I have had if I did not have a few good mentors along the way. At almost every step during each of my careers I have had a strong mentor. A mentor is someone who has your best interest in mind when they are mentoring. They will not have an ulterior motive or a hidden agenda. A true mentor will be looking out for you and is driven by the desire to help. As a leader you should be a mentor, and driven to help the people on your team because it benefits them.

A mentor will be able to observe the behavior of others and provide feedback to the mentee. Many times, at least in my own life, my struggles are self-imposed, caused by my perceptions and paradigms, and a mentor was able to help me see and understand that. As a mentor you are not blinded by another person's paradigms, although you do have to be concerned about your own. In my experience, mentors have been able to identify my paradigms and help me see past them and make the changes needed to get the results I desire.

As a leader, I have been a mentor to many people, either formally or informally. Recently I was working with an individual, Scott, and I asked him about his professional goal. Scott had been a fairly successful engineer; he had risen up the engineering ladder rather quickly and was filling a team leadership role. I was introduced to Scott when his management chain recommended him for mentoring in management. I love to mentor so I agreed to meet with him. On our first meeting I told Scott that I wasn't the kind of mentor who was going to focus on how he should do his job or what job assignment he should take next. Although I would give him some advice where needed I wanted to focus our conversations on what his goals were and how he could achieve them. I assumed he already knew how to be a successful engineer and an effective leader, or he wouldn't have been in his job and had someone actively looking to find him a mentor. I decided I wanted to help him realize his professional goals and take the necessary actions to accomplish those goals. We'd work on the specifics of his job as part of the process for goal achievement. Scott agreed that he liked this approach to a mentoring relationship and we agreed to meet regularly.

When Scott told me about his goals, he said he wanted to be in a profit and loss position in the company. I related, as I once had that same goal. I asked him the follow-up question: at what level? He told me he wanted to do this at the director level, to which I responded why not as a vice president? He thought being a director was more realistic. I immediately challenged him and explained that it was his belief system and his paradigms that were determining what was realistic. He still had plenty of years ahead of him before he reached retirement age and there was no reason he couldn't get that far in his career. I saw the light come on here.

At this time, Scott was in an engineering role, and not even in an engineering management position, although he was a team lead. Because of this, I had to ask him what is plans were to move into a program management position. In his company program managers are responsible for profit and loss, while engineering supplies the people resources to execute the programs. He was thinking he'd do what he was doing for the next four or five years because he thought he had to wait that long. Aha! Another paradigm that was holding him back! I left him with the question: if you really want to be responsible for a profit and loss division, why wait four or five years to start down that path?

That same day, I presented him with some job opportunities in the program management department so he could start thinking about his options. I don't think until this point he was actively looking for opportunities. When he saw the opportunities, he realized that he was indeed qualified for a program management role, and there happened to be one that he was interested in applying for. Much to my delight the next time we met, when I asked how things were going, he told me that he had applied for and was accepted to one of the positions I'd sent over to him. At this point Scott was excited about his new career path, and of course I felt good that I was able to help someone essentially accelerate their career by four or five years just by asking some thought-provoking questions.

For me, the most effective mentor I ever had was my father. He was a mentor in the truest sense of the word: his true desire for me was only to see me succeed. As much as I would like to say that I've never made mistakes, I wouldn't be where I am today without learning some valuable lessons, many the hard way, and my father was there through all of them.

When I was in high school I used to pride myself on being an athlete. I played football, but my favorite sport was basketball. My sophomore year in high school, I dislocated my shoulder playing football, and eventually this required surgery to repair. I was unable to play sports that year, and that became a real struggle for me. Up until the injury I had a goal and a vision of myself playing college basketball. I had a lot of work to do, but I was working toward that goal. When I sustained the injury to my shoulder, I perceived this as a showstopper to me achieving my goals. After the surgery, I was not only a year behind my peers in development, but I has also lost some of the range of motion in my shoulder. I eventually allowed this injury to become an excuse to quit pursuing my dream of playing college basketball, and by extension I failed. Without the discipline of the sports routine, I developed some bad habits and some unhealthy relationships.

While all this was happening, my father wasn't shy about pointing out where the road I was traveling would lead. I would find myself in undesirable situations from time to time, and he would be there to help me see a way to clean up whatever situation I was in. He was there the entire time, and I am sure it wasn't pleasant for him. He would offer advice when he could, but I was a teenager so I already knew everything and I was going to have to make my own mistakes. Because he did give me advice along the way, and pointed out the right path, and where I went astray, I was able to learn from my mistakes. He had the foresight to understand that I had to make my own mistakes, and he was there to help me to learn from them. Being a father now, I understand that it would have been difficult to fight the desire to just say "do it my way!" but he understood that I wouldn't learn from that. Fortunately for me, the mistakes I made were relatively minor in the grand scheme of things, probably because of the influence of my father.

Eventually, though, I started getting tired of learning life lessons the hard way and decided I needed a new direction in my life. I looked no further than the only mentor I had, which was my father. I decided to follow in his footsteps and enlisted in the Navy at the age of 19. My father was a Navy veteran, and I always admired that about him, so when I needed new direction it seemed logical that I would follow in his footsteps. You can probably imagine his reaction when I came home one day and told him I had enlisted. I can remember the look on his face: it was a combination of pride that I was following in his footsteps and relief that I was going to get the discipline I needed.

The night before I was going to be picked up for boot camp, I couldn't sleep. I was terrified. I was about to go way outside of my comfort zone. The funny thing was I enlisted, I wanted to go to the Navy, nobody forced the decision upon me, but nevertheless when it came down to it I was scared. I was sitting in my parent's family room with some late-night show on TV. It made no difference what was on; I wasn't watching it. I was sitting alone in the dark watching TV because I was too scared to sleep. My father must have either heard the TV or needed a glass of water, because he came downstairs and sat with me until the recruiter came to pick me up. He told me how proud he was, that I was making the right decision. He told me of the friendships he made and the adventures he had while in the Navy. He encouraged me and helped me follow through on the decision to actually go into the Navy. Again, his only motive was to help me be the best person I could be. He was there for me when I needed help the most, and to this day he continues to encourage me and helps me to recognize when I am getting in my own way.

I can certainly point to other instances where a mentor or a coach has helped me achieve my goals. But mentorship cannot be a one-way street, and everyone should be obligated to give back and provide mentorship to whoever can use your help. This does not have to be any type of formal relationship. I know that some companies formalize these things, but I believe that someone that is senior in their job taking time to answer the questions of a junior employee is a form of mentorship. In my staff meetings I like to talk lessons learned or provide guidance on topics that I know my teams are struggling with. These are all forms of mentorship. Providing useful advice, solicited or unsolicited, is mentoring, and mentoring is the responsibility of leadership to pass along that knowledge and advice to help the next generation of the workforce become successful.

The "A" Team and "C" Team Myth

What makes some teams succeed and others with seemingly similar talent fail? The answer is quite simple: it is all about leadership. I have been associated with many teams in my career, and leadership makes the difference. From my research and experience, I don't believe there are "A" teams and "C" teams, but "A" leaders and "C" leaders.

It is a leader's job and responsibility to make sure that they have all the right players on their team. Leaders are responsible for identifying, developing, and retaining talent for their respective teams. In addition to putting the right players on the team, a leader's other job is to ensure that everyone is working toward the same goal and believes in the end product. If any of these aspects are missing, then the team is not able to function at maximum capacity and is therefore falling short of its potential.

The leader is responsible for articulating a vision and defining the goals and strategy for the team to accomplish success, regardless of who is on the team. You can have an extremely talented team assembled, but if they do not all have complementary skills and talents then you may not have the right skills to be successful. There is a commercial I saw on TV one time—I think it was for some sort of investment service. The firm was talking about the importance of diversity by having two golfers getting ready to go play a round. One of the golfers has a bag full of different drivers, and of course the other golfer has the standard set of clubs. Now you don't have to be an avid golfer to understand that if you have a bag with all the same clubs you won't necessarily have the equipment needed to be successful during the round. It would be the same thing if a mechanic went to work on your car and only had a toolbox full of screwdrivers. Sure he can accomplish one task pretty well, but what happens when he needs a wrench?

I have seen teams, and actually led teams, that at different stages in their existence were considered A teams and C teams. One example is when I took over a small project of a software support program. This job was to help provide software upgrades for a delivered system that was going through its final integration stages on the end platform. OK, so that might sound vague or complicated for a non-engineer, so I will give you an analogy. We have all been on an airplane and understand there are several systems on an airplane, such as navigation systems, flight control systems, communication systems, entertainment systems, etc. All of these systems have software that is typically developed at someone's desk and tested in a laboratory or on a prototype before it is installed on an aircraft. This is done because it is easier to fix a bug if found earlier than later. But eventually all the systems have to be put on the airplane and tested. Sometimes there are interactions or something that is unique on an airplane that can't be fully replicated in a lab. The program I was working with was in this final stage of testing and my team was responsible for successfully fixing and testing new fixes and sending new software to the customer.

I had a team of two engineers, and until I was brought on board, they really didn't have anyone overseeing the engineering aspects of the program. They were asked to go fix something and tell me when they were done. That might be overly simplistic, but basically that gets to the point. As you can imagine they had issues with incomplete testing, and maybe not providing a fully implemented solution to the problem. By all accounts this would be considered a C team. They were getting work done, but not necessarily the best quality of work. I came in, added new members to the team to help fill in some gaps, laid out my vision for the projects ahead of us, and got everyone on board. We started meeting and exceeding customer expectations, and we were producing products of higher quality than ever before. This happened in less than one year. At the end of the year, when these engineers received their performance reviews, they received higher scores than previous years and even received bonuses for their efforts. Same engineers, same task, different results, all because of a change in leadership.

Hero Mentality

I have seen too many examples of where the success of a project was dependent on one individual. Typically this one individual would have a particular skill or talent and therefore would be in demand for that one skill or talent. I have worked in large companies where we have many projects going on at the same time, and it would never cease to amaze me that all these projects would rely on the same people. The justification for this was that nobody else had the skill to get the job done. So the success of a program would rest on the availability of one individual; this person would fly in with their red cape to save the day and be a hero. Wow, what happens when this person wins the lottery and retires early? Well, honestly the chances of someone winning the lottery are something in the ballpark of 1 in 75 million, so we can probably take that chance, right? Wrong! People retire all the time, get sick, a spouse get relocated, or they decide to change careers. Relying on one person is dangerous.

I found that oftentimes the problem was with the leadership. First and foremost, nobody was born being great at their job; they all worked at it and learned it. So therefore someone else can learn it too. It is leadership's responsibility to identify talent and provide the proper training and experiences to avoid this hero mentality.

Leaders need to be focused on growing the next generation of talent to ensure future success. If the right forethought is put into choosing whom to select for a stretch assignment, to fill in for the hero, the results can be quite surprising. At one point when I was a functional manager responsible for providing staff to programs, I had a program manager tell me he needed a particular engineer on his program. At this time that person was not available so I offered someone I thought was a gifted and talented engineer, but didn't have as much experience in the particular area, or that particular product that the program manager thought he needed. After some convincing, the program manager reluctantly agreed that the engineer I was offering would be acceptable. Two months later when I needed the engineer for another assignment, that program manager would not let him go. He excelled in that position and exceeded everyone's expectations.

As leaders we need to be continuously looking forward to growing talent (keeping our people and ourselves challenged and stretched) if we truly intend to avoid the hero mentality and maximize the potential of those around us. Remember the hero became the hero because someone pushed them and put them in situations to learn and grow—it is our responsibility to see that opportunity afforded to as many people as possible. This is why identifying talent is such a crucial part of growing success.

Shared Results

I have used sports analogies during my writing to help illustrate the benefits of good teamwork, and that is not an accident. In addition to being a great way to draw an analogy, I learned very valuable lessons while I was playing sports, specifically team sports. In order to have a strong and valuable workforce, you need to build an effective and efficient team. In my mind a team has two objectives: first, a team is a group of people working toward a common goal, and second, a team is a group of people who share the results of the team effort. A professional football team starts out the season intending to win the Super Bowl. If that is not their goal for the year, they'll never be able to win the Super Bowl, and that statement goes back to the concept of visualization. Through the season the team works together, everyone from the members of the team selected to the Pro Bowl (the all-stars) to the guys playing on the practice squad. Every member of the team understands that their individual success is tied to the success of the team. And when a team wins the Super Bowl, it is not just the team members that played that Sunday that participate in the parades, the celebrations, and that get a ring—the entire team does. They all understand that it was a group effort to accomplish the goal, and not on the shoulders of any individual player or coach.

In the business world, a culture of shared results has to be prevalent and understood to achieve the highest levels of success. Every member of the team is responsible for their results, and the team's results; it is not productive to blame someone else for not achieving results. Within a culture of shared results everyone in the company benefits from shared success or the effects of shared failures. When a culture of shared results is prevalent in an organization, the positive effects are staggering. Help comes from all angles, and amazing things are accomplished.

Success belongs to your team, but the failures are yours. As a leader of a team you are responsible for building the team and leading them to victory. There will be issues along the way, but ultimately the outcome is your responsibly. As a leader you cannot deflect the responsibility and you cannot pass blame. If you are the leader of the team you own the failure.

When your team is successful, they deserve all the credit. After all, they are the individuals that came together and did the work. To use another sports example, during a professional football game the coach of the team makes no blocks, doesn't tackle anyone, makes no passes, he doesn't catch a single pass, nor does he even touch a football during the course of a game. The coach is on the sideline giving direction, adjusting his plan, and evaluating the circumstances on the field. When the team wins, the coach cannot stand up at a press conference and start saying, "I did a great job today! My game plan was spectacular and can you believe that catch I had to score the winning touchdown!" The reason he cannot take credit for the success is because he didn't do the work to execute the plan. The leader, in this case the coach, did put in motion the plans and preparation necessary for the members of the team to be successful, and he also recruited and developed the talent on his team, but the coach did not directly produce the success.

Conversely, when a team fails to be successful, the coach cannot stand up and say that his team members failed to execute the plan, or that the wrong players were on the field and that is why they lost. There is no evidence that the plan was the right plan to begin with. The coach may have produced a bad plan or did not have the proper personnel to execute the plan. Additionally, it is the coach's job to put in place the practice and preparation needed to be successful on the field. If the team is unsuccessful the failure lies squarely on the coach's shoulders.

CHAPTER 7
Maximize Your Potential

Success will come through the absolute belief that you can achieve whatever it is you want to achieve. It does not matter what you've accomplished this far in your life. It doesn't matter where you are from, your education level, or who your parents were. Success comes from a decision to go after whatever you want, the determination to accomplish your dreams, and the commitment to push through any adversity along the way.

When watching TV, I often see commercials for investment firms. In these commercials the firms will brag about how well their mutual funds do and how well their investors do by investing with them. However, at the end of these commercials they show the fine print, which states, "The SEC requires funds to tell investors that a fund's past performance does not necessarily predict future results."

Now, these investment firms write this as a get out of jail free clause. If you choose to invest with this firm and you do not achieve the same results the firm can claim that they stated that there was risk and that past performance does not guarantee future success. Although the statement is used to protect investment firms from lawsuits from dissatisfied customers, they are 100% correct. Past performance is not an indicator of future success. Present thinking is an indicator of future success, especially in life. From the law of attraction we know that what you are predominately thinking about now is what you will bring about in your future. What you condition your subconscious mind to attract you will bring into your life. If you change what you are focusing on now, you can change what your future outcome will be.

In the introduction to this book I stated that the theories in this book are based on the fact that life is not a series of random events that happen but a series of events that you cause to happen. In order to fully maximize your potential, you need to cause things to happen in your life that will enable you to start achieving success greater than any successes you ever achieved thus far in your life.

The first step to maximizing your potential is to start thinking differently. Much of the research I have done directly indicates that successful people think differently than the average person. Successful people have unwavering faith in their own abilities to accomplish great tasks and do not rely on others for their own success. They will hold a vision of what they want to accomplish in their lives and back up that vision with the utmost belief and faith that they will accomplish what they set out to accomplish.

Earlier in this book, I spoke about Petty Officer Swank and the successes he was able to achieve in his Navy career. Swank was able to achieve these successes because he had the belief, despite what others were telling him, that he could be successful as an aviation electronics technician. He had faith that if he worked hard, studied, and learned his trade that he'd be able to succeed. I do not think it is a mere coincidence that a man with that level of faith and determination was also able to be a strong leader. Swank projected his belief system on the rest of us, and as a result we were all able to accomplish more in our own personal development.

Successful people have a different level of awareness than most people. For example, most of us follow the same routines in life that our neighbors, colleagues, and parents followed. We would go to school, get a job with the hope that if we were good at our jobs, we would be rewarded with promotions and pay increases. Oftentimes, somewhere along the line we seem to plateau, find ourselves comfortable, and the drive to achieve more diminishes. At this point we tend to accept the status quo, because it is easy and predictable, and rationalize this as some level of success.

To be successful you have to change that thought process; you have to change your expectations and you have to change your paradigm. This is not necessarily an easy thing to do, because your paradigm has been programmed starting the day you were born. If your parents believed that life was meant to be a struggle and any job is a good job, chances are you believe (or at some point believed) the same. You might be able to think differently in your conscious mind, but I suspect your conscious mind and your paradigms are not always in agreement. One test to know if your paradigm is in line with your conscious thought is to think about quitting your job to pursue something else. I mean really think about it and get emotionally involved with the idea, not dream about it. When you think about it do you immediately start thinking of reasons you can't quit your job and pursue what you want? Does this thought scare you and make you uncomfortable? If so, that is your paradigm holding you back. The new job would interfere with the sense of security you have in your present situation. You need to change your paradigm. Think about it for a second: do you really have security in your present job? What happens if the company faces a downturn or there is a merger with a competitor? Would your job be at risk then?

If I have been able to convince you that changing your paradigm is necessary, then you are probably asking, "How do I do that?" Well, you programmed your paradigm once, you just need to start programming it again, and this time with the program you choose!

Develop Your Vision

I spent a lot of time in this book talking about the subconscious mind and visualization. Develop a vision of you providing goods and services that are needed. Picture in your mind what your life will look like when you are providing those goods and services to other people.

The first step in changing your paradigm is to develop your vision. Spend time to give some deliberate thought to what your vision is and begin to form mental pictures in your mind. Repeat this often, until you have filled in all the details of every aspect of your life. You should be able to run a movie in your mind of what you want your life to look like from the moment you wake up in the morning to the time you go to bed. Picture yourself starting your day feeling excited about what you will do that day. Picture what the bedroom in your house will look like. Imagine driving to work in the car you desire. Visualize the interior of the car, the music you'll listen to. Go even further to picture your office when you get to work, and imagine dealing with the people you work with. Imagine your service or product being sold and your customers benefitting from your work. Imagine the dinners and vacations you will enjoy when you are living in your dream world. Even after you get all the details worked out replay this over and over in your mind like watching your favorite movie.

Because a picture is worth a thousand words, when I created my visions I would oftentimes find a picture of a house that I would want, or a car that I would want, and create a collage of the images of what my future would look like. This is actually a common technique and they are referred to as vision boards. The mind actually works in pictures, and this can be demonstrated by asking you to tell me about an event or object in your life; you will first replay the event or see the object in your mind and then describe the picture, or as Van Gough would say, you dream the picture then describe the picture. I would keep the pictures I created where I would regularly see them to make sure I would keep the images fresh in my mind.

I am also of the belief that your vision should be aligned with your talent and interests. Although you can learn new skills and talents, aligning your talents and interests with your vision will help you stay motivated toward achieving your goals. If you are good at something, it tends to be more fun, so the work necessary to achieve your goal won't feel as much like work. Also, if you are working toward something that you are interested in dedicating your energy to, achieving your goal will also be easy.

Take advantage of any free time you have to watch the movie of your future self. Opportunities such as waiting for an appointment or just before you go to bed are perfect times to replay this movie. Repeating your own movie in your mind and getting emotionally involved with these movies will impress the images on your subconscious, which will in turn put you in harmony with the things you desire, and through the law of attraction the things you desire will begin to present themselves to you in the physical world.

Risk

All great achievements involve risk; therefore in order to maximize your potential you have to take and accept risks. If you are not going out on that limb, if you are not accepting that kind of challenge, then you are not going to accomplish anything great. Manned space flight involved risk, and at times that risk was realized, but we have put a man on the moon and continuously inhabit a space station orbiting the earth. Because of these risks, we now have satellite communications sending us television programming from around the world. Long-distance phone calls are commonplace where 30 years ago they were expensive and occurred less frequently. Thomas Edison took risks to invent the electric light bulb, and people claimed that Marconi was insane when he presented his theory of radio waves and subsequently invented the radio. Today electric light and radios are commonplace in every house.

For most people taking risks goes against many of our instincts, especially those of us who have any kind of project management experience or training. When learning project management skills, we learn three ways to deal with risk: avoidance, transfer, or mitigation. If at all possible, we like to execute projects and avoid risks, and on the surface this makes sense; if we do something risky and fail we will probably struggle to meet project objectives. If we can't avoid the risk, we may want to transfer the risk, so we set up contracts that transfer the cost of risks to the customer or even hire subcontractors to handle the higher-risk areas and therefore transfer the responsibly (i.e., the cost of the risk) to someone else. If a risk cannot be avoided or transferred, the next step is to mitigate it. When mitigating a risk, we look for steps we can take to help ensure that the risk is not realized.

In reality we all take risks every day and most of the time we don't think twice about it. More accurately, pretty much everything we do involves some level of risk, and it is up to all of us to evaluate the risk versus the reward. For example, when we get in our cars to go to work or run errands, there is risk that we could get in a car accident, yet we are comfortable with taking that risk. Partially because we have driven to work or to the store countless times and been successful, the risk is perceived to be low.

Maximizing the human potential means taking risks in your own life. The risks you have to make must be large and daring. Staying in your comfort zone and continuing to work in areas that you are comfortable in is the definition of complacency. However, that reality is a limitation in your own mind. Once you can conceive of something larger, once you have faith that you can achieve more, once you open your mind to a larger reality, then and only then can you maximize your potential and achieve higher and higher levels of success.

Career coaches that help people achieve higher levels of success in their careers teach that in order to get to the next level, you need to learn to think at a higher level. The skills and talents needed to succeed in your present position are not necessarily the skills needed to be successful at the next higher level. I had experience and successes as a project manager and leader of technical teams in my previous career. Toward the end of my career it was obvious to me that the skills that helped me be successful in my career were not the skills that would drive me to executive management. How did I know that? Because the executive management teams were not the people who were executing the programs. Their view was much larger than the view required to do my job. Had I just focused on being a great leader of technical teams, then I would never have advanced past that stage of my career.

Change Your Paradigms

When you have fully impressed your vision onto your subconscious mind and the things you desire are starting to appear in your life, you have to be ready to recognize the opportunity and take action to seize it. This is when you will hear an inner voice begin to raise doubt and tell you that it is not the right time or raise questions as to the validity of your decision. This is your paradigm causing you to think this way. Taking advantage of an opportunity that will take you out of your comfort zone will likely be in direct conflict with your paradigm. You will begin to feel doubt and fear. This is completely natural, and we have all experienced this at some point in our lives. I know that I was nervous and scared when I joined the Navy. The world I entered was completely different than what I experienced. Although I knew that enlisting in the Navy was something I wanted to do, and I had chosen to do it, but it didn't stop my paradigm from causing anxiety. I had similar fears when I left the company I was working for in Houston and started a new job in a new state. Although I wasn't happy with the job, I was employed and I was comfortable. I had to change my paradigm by overcoming these fears and doing what I thought was the right thing to do.

Your paradigm will cause fear and anxiety whenever you try to introduce something into your life that contradicts your paradigm. In other words, when you take action that seems to conflict with the programmed sense of reality you have used to define your world.

However, once you muster the courage to go against your paradigm and take the next step, you will find that this new world will become your new paradigm. The Navy became my new paradigm. Ironically, as much as I wanted to get out of the Navy, when my enlistment was nearly over I was contemplating extending my enlistment and perhaps making a career out of the Navy. My intention prior to that was to take advantage of the GI Bill and go to college, but when it came time to execute that decision, my paradigm wanted to guide me into staying in the Navy because I was comfortable, and going home introduced uncertainty. Each time I made a decision that caused anxiety, and I had the courage to persevere, the rewards were much more than if I had stayed in my previous paradigm.

Goals

When most of us set goals, we set goals that we know we can accomplish. In our workplaces we are likely to set a goal to get the next promotion, stay in that position for a given period of time, and then look for the next position. I know in my life, I had taken certain positions at work, where I did that for a while and then looked for the next position. The new position would often be similar to the job I currently had, but perhaps with a larger scope of responsibility. In reality I was just doing more of the same, and it wasn't really challenging me.

I watched most of my peers follow a similar pattern. The company I worked for encouraged this, as it presented the least risk for them as well. If they saw I was a capable team leader, it wasn't a stretch to convince someone that I could take on a larger lead role. It was a harder sell to convince hiring managers that I was also capable of managing departments.

Compensation

In order to maximize the human potential, we should all be continuously looking for advancement in our lives. We should strive to advance in education, experience, and our contribution to society. I believe it is a disservice for you to deny yourself the opportunities for advancement in all areas of your life.

To advance in life and in your career you need to make yourself fill a bigger space than the one you already occupy. For me it is easiest to think of this concept in terms of the relationships we have in our lives. When you choose a person as your significant other, you chose that person because they fill a space in your life larger than all of your other friends. The companionship is more pleasurable, and the relationship is more meaningful. As a result you want to spend more time with that person, share more things with that person, and when things work out, you will decide to spend your life with that person.

The same concept is true with your life ambitions. Whether you work for a large company, small company, or are selling your services on the open market, to be highly successful you need to fill a role or provide a service that is larger than what you already are providing. The key is to raise your level of awareness and begin to act and perform as if you were at a higher level. Take your present situation out of your calculations, act and work to the best of your ability every day, and always try to provide service above what is required of you to perform your present duties. If you can make your boss's job easier or your customers experience more beneficial to them than just the service you provide, you are beginning to work at a higher level of awareness. When you start to work and perform with these higher levels of awareness, it is then that new and larger opportunities will begin to present themselves.

There are three basic factors that determine your value to any workplace. These factors dictate how much money you make, and in the corporate setting they will dictate your position in the organization.

Is there a need for what you do? Do you provide a service that is critical for the company or your customers to be successful? If you are currently employed or are currently making money selling goods or services, there is obviously some need for what you do. Companies and individuals will pay you if you provide a service they feel is valuable. If you do not provide a meaningful service, or when your service is no longer required, then your value goes down.

The second contributor is based on your ability to perform your job or service. Are you good at what you do? Are you the best at what you do? Being mediocre at your job doesn't demand higher pay or advancement for your present contribution. One way to increase your value to your company or employers is to become the absolute best at what you do.

The third factor is based on how much difficulty your employers or customers would have if they had to find someone else to provide the service you perform. When you do something that is needed, and you are the best at it, this kind of falls in line. But when you are working your way up to become the best, this is more of a challenge. This is where it is important to provide more service than you are presently paid to provide. I have seen situations where someone on a team leaves to pursue other opportunities for one reason or another and when that person leaves it takes a combination of two or three people to fill the role that was vacated. Conversely, there have been other times when someone leaves a team, and later it is determined that a backfill wasn't needed. Now assuming that these people didn't leave because the job was no longer required, one person clearly was harder to replace than the other, and was therefore more valuable.

The level of success you achieve is a direct effect of how well you understand and utilize the three factors above. In order to change the effects or results you are presently experiencing, or achieve more success, you have to understand and change what is causing the effects that you are experiencing. If you are already successful, it would be beneficial for you to understand what is making you successful so you can continue to enjoy the results that are making you successful. We all know the definition of insanity is repeating the same behavior and expecting different results. When you begin to model your behavior based on those three factors, then by default the results will have to change.

Continuous Improvement

I know many people who are good at what they do. I know many people who make a comfortable living doing what they do. Because these people are good at what they do and are making a comfortable living doing it, they do not push to get better. Sure, they become more efficient in their work over time simply by repetition, but there is no real improvement in their skills. At times this depresses me, because I clearly see these people as not striving to achieve their maximum potential. They accept the status quo, and then I will hear them complain when merit is handed out and they receive little or nothing, but they've come to accept this as reality and do not take any action to remedy the situation.

As I stated above, the second factor in your compensation is your ability to provide a service. Are you the best at what you do? Really consider that question, as I am sure many of us are really good at our jobs, but are you the best? If not, what are you doing to become the best? Over the last several years, I decided I wanted to be recognized as a role model and teacher of leadership principles. I followed the principles described in this book, and I first envisioned myself as a strong leader. I would hear stories of people who were influenced by great leaders and people who would follow those leaders almost anywhere. I wanted to be one of those leaders. Furthermore, I wasn't going to be satisfied with just being one of those leaders; I wanted to teach others to become strong leaders themselves.

When I made that decision I started reading and studying the principles of self-improvement and leadership characteristics. I would deliberately change my behavior to incorporate the ideas I was learning and practice the skills needed to become a better leader. After several years of studying and sharpening my leadership skills, I was finally recognized for my leadership skills.

The key takeaway to the story of Jekel's Law of Human Dynamics is to not always take the path of least resistance, and sometimes look to take the road less traveled. Look around at your peers, and strive to find ways to do things differently. Do not rationalize as "nobody else is doing it." If you do what everyone else is doing, you will get the same results everyone else is getting. Taking the road less traveled will and should oftentimes be in direct conflict with your paradigm and will make you uncomfortable, and that is a good thing. Every time you have the courage to step out of your comfort zone and defy your paradigm, you will grow. Success comes from being able to outgrow your present position in life and take on that higher level of success.

CHAPTER 8
Maximize the Potential of Your Team

LEADERSHIP IS SO important in maximizing potential because effective leaders also raise the performance of those around them. Helping your team members maximize their full potential is important because when everyone is executing and performing at their maximum potential the productivity of the team improves, and in the end everyone will succeed. This is a win-win scenario because when your team wins you win!

The same principles that apply to maximizing your own potential apply to maximizing your team's potential. It focuses around vision and leadership. You are not necessarily required to have everyone on your team understand the difference between the conscious and subconscious mind; however, you do want to instill a vision and encourage them to adapt the same vision. You will want to help them overcome the barriers of their own mind and to take risks.

Only by maximizing your team's potential will you be able to maximize your own potential.

Having a clear and concise vision of where you want to go and the types of successes you want to achieve allows the power of your subconscious mind to draw upon the law of attraction to bring about exactly what you were envisioning.

Management Philosophy

In any organization the leadership and management team is responsible for making their company profitable. They are required to continuously look for ways to improve profit margins and efficiencies and identify new products for the company to pursue to continue to grow. The executive leaders are responsible for defining strategy for future growth, to evaluate product line development and adjacent markets to penetrate, and where to invest internal funds. These strategies need to be in line with the skills and capabilities of the workforce, so that growth is organic and not a struggle.

Additionally all levels of management have a responsibility to build a culture of loyalty through loyalty. This happens when management empowers the entire workforce to make decisions within their scope of responsibility, ask questions when they do not understand something, and make suggestions when appropriate. When a workforce takes these actions, it is also the responsibility of management to respond appropriately. When a workforce does not trust that their management will listen to their ideas, or will undermine lower-level decisions, morale is diminished and productivity will necessarily and proportionally decrease. Good ideas can come from anywhere, and a good idea that results in action is better than a great idea that does not.

Everyone on your team has an obligation to do their part to ensure team success. Everyone on the team must feel it necessary to take action to improve profitability. All team members are expected to give full attention to the tasks at hand, be accountable for their own actions, and take responsibility for achieving success. Everyone at all levels in an organization should hold themselves, peers, and managers accountable for their actions.

My leadership philosophy has always been centered on creating a motivated and empowered workforce. This is accomplished by building loyalty through loyalty. To ensure success, it is imperative that the workforce believes the leadership team is there to support them in their daily activities. Likewise, it is equally important the leadership team believes everyone in the organization has the company's best interest in mind. This frees up the leadership team from tending to the day-to-day activities and allows them to focus and act more strategically. It is this mutual loyalty through all levels of a company that will drive the types of success that causes some companies to be the best in their respective industries.

One of the strongest discriminators between companies is the effectiveness of their workforce. All companies can put out a mission statement and hire talented employees, but successful companies excel at creating an engaged and motivated workforce. Most companies understand this, although I have observed executive management take steps that discourage a highly engaged workforce. Instead I hear that leadership is about making tough decisions, which typically means a decision that negatively impacts the morale of their teams. I fully agree that a leader has to make tough decisions; however, it is my experience that in many cases the tougher decision is to invest in your team members for long-term mutual benefit. Leaders have to be focused on creating a culture within a team that truly makes the team a place where all the team members choose to work and not just show up for a paycheck. When this culture is created employees will naturally give that extra discretionary effort to ensure project success. The importance of leaders to create an atmosphere of success by creating and building a culture of loyalty through loyalty can't be understated.

As a leader, I have found that success comes from a conscious effort to continuously and diligently help the person sitting next to me. Success does not come from any one person's actions alone, and therefore leaders should be focused on helping everyone they come into contact with to maximize their effectiveness regardless of their position in the organization. This means helping customers, direct reports, peers, and superiors excel in their own tasks and maximize their contributions to their respective assignments. Leaders should develop a habit of continuously working with their teams to make helping others a focus in their daily activities and rewarding those who make efforts in this area.

Whenever I have been assigned to take over as a leader for a new group, one of the first things I would do is have a staff meeting and at that meeting I would try to accomplish a few things. One, I would introduce myself and give a little of my background so my new team would know who I am and where I get my frame of reference. This gives my team members insight into my personal paradigm and a reference point for how I make decisions. Once I would do that I would tell the team where I am planning to take the team, and usually this is a pretty simple statement along the lines of "I am going to take this team to achieve successes we never thought possible." This is fairly generic and open to interpretation for each member to internalize what that means to them. Finally I lay out my principles and guides for how I make decisions. Here is where I tell the team the importance of helping the person sitting next to them and asking for help when you need help. I express to them that I am their partner in this, and that I will always be on their side when they need an advocate.

The vision I have for my teams has always been to look at each other as team members, and be able to rely on the person sitting next to them. As their leader, I am always there when needed, and asking me for help will be a positive experience.

Articulate Your Vision

Just as important as it is to have your vision you must be able to clearly articulate your vision to those you want to follow you. You will not inspire anyone to follow you if they do not know where you are going as a leader and why it benefits them. Our founding fathers made it clear that they were creating a new government, for the people and by the people. President Lincoln had a vision to abolish slavery and to restore and preserve the Union. President Kennedy was going to send a man to the moon when he jumped into the space race with the USSR.

> *We choose to go to the moon in this decade and do the other things, not because they are easy, but because they are hard.*
> —John F. Kennedy, 35th president of the United States

These people were great leaders because they had visions and could clearly articulate these visions for people to follow. Without people following these leaders and their visions, we might still be British subjects, we might still suffer the atrocities of slavery, or we might still be lagging behind the USSR in the space race, and the Cold War might still be going on.

When articulating your vision to those you choose to lead, you have to present a clear picture of what the end game looks like. People need to understand why they want to go where you want to take them. Your vision should answer some simple questions:

- How is your vision of the future better than what we have now?
- When we reach the end game, who benefits and how does this help me?
- What is my responsibility?

Being able to clearly define the objectives of your vision will ensure you have full buy-in from the people you intend to lead and that they are committed to going along for the ride. People will not be inspired if they do not understand where they are going or understand why they are going there.

Communicate Expectations

Part of articulating your visions is to clearly communicate the expectations you have for everyone on your team. If you cannot effectively communicate your expectations to your team they don't have a chance of doing what you expect them to do. For a supervisor communicating expectations is not just about meeting with team members and setting goals for the year in January and reviewing those goals during the year. A leader should have expectations for how they want members of their team to act and define the rules that will be used for making decisions. After all, your team is a reflection and an extension of you. Leaders need their team members to be acting in accordance with the values that the leader thinks are important.

There are many ways to communicate expectations, and not everyone responds to the same form of communication; therefore I have communicated expectations to my employees in a wide variety of ways. The most common form of setting expectations was to do our annual goal-setting. This was the only form of communication required by my company. I would meet with my team members early in the year, usually in January or February, to set their goals for the year. It was here we would talk about what was expected in terms of job performance, and what tasks everyone was required to do. Midway through the year we would meet again to discuss progress on the goals, and then at the end of the year each employee would be evaluated on how they performed against their goals and expectations.

Another method I took advantage of was to conduct regular staff meetings. I used staff meetings to pass along department news and announcements. I shared information that came from my boss, and of course I would go around the room to understand what each team member was working on and what challenges they were having so I could offer help if needed. However, and probably most importantly, I used this time to lay out my expectations. I used slides for my staff meetings, mostly because it forced me to be disciplined enough to prepare before the staff meeting, and I always had slides talking about the importance of teamwork and helping others. I used quotes from famous people to drive home specific points, and I would lay out a specific goal that I was working on at that point in time and talk about what that meant to them.

I would also have regular one-on-one meetings with my employees. These one-on-one meetings were usually conducted monthly, more frequently if needed, and I would typically set aside 30 minutes to meet with my employees. I would ignore my email and phone calls. This time was 100% dedicated to the person sitting in my office. I would have no agenda for these meetings, and I would use the time to listen to what the employee was struggling with or needed help with. I would use this time to coach, guide, and mentor on the topic of their choice. Oftentimes I would be asked to explain the rationale behind certain decisions or help the person work though a problem. These one-on-one sessions were important because coaching and mentoring are important to me, and since I expect those characteristics from my direct reports, it is important that I lead by example.

Occasionally there would be a policy change or an incident that necessitated that a message be reinforced. For example, during one assignment the department I was supporting had a history of delivering products to our customer that were not fully tested and shortcuts were taken in documenting the pedigree of the products in order to minimize cost. Predictably there were failures in the field that should have been caught with proper testing and documentation, and this prompted the engineering director to clearly define the policies and procedures for delivering the product. I was in full support of this policy and wanted to make sure my team fully understood the policy. When emphasizing the importance of adhering to policy and procedures, I would typically send out the information in an email because I could guarantee everyone on my staff received the email and had a written record of the policy for reference. In addition to the email stating the policy, I would also address the policy in a staff meeting to highlight the importance and to allow my team to ask questions.

In addition to email, staff meetings, and annual goal setting and follow up, I would walk around to see my team members on a regular basis. I would see them several times a week, in their offices, cubes or in the laboratory. This would give me an opportunity to see what they were working on first hand and see the problems. I developed this habit after a few years in leadership and found that this was probably the most powerful tool that I had at my disposal, and by doing this I was able to develop a level of trust with my direct reports. I would not always have a particular agenda to discuss, so I would often show up and just ask what they were doing and if they needed any help. But going to their workspace showed that they were important to me, as they weren't just being summoned to the boss's office when I wanted to know how things were going. An added benefit is I got to know them on a more personal level by observing what was on their desks. I could see a family picture and ask how old the kids were or see a coffee mug from a college and ask how their kids are doing at school. These are small things, but more personal than I can get at a staff meeting, allowing me to connect better with my team. This was another way that I could build a trusting relationship, which builds the foundation for a loyal team.

Treat Everyone with Respect

A great leader treats everyone with respect. A great leader will listen to everyone's opinion, from the most senior person on the team to the new guy on his first day. The struggle at times is to get people to honestly express their opinions, especially if it goes against the crowd. A junior person on the team may have an opinion opposite of the most senior guy, and might be right. If this person isn't able to express his opinion, then the best ideas might not be considered.

In order to effectively treat everyone fairly you have to get to know your team on a personal level. Learn what motivates the people on your team and what they do in their spare time and what they do on the weekends. When you show you care about members on your team, the trust level goes exponentially up. For me, there were some simple things that I would do. When I was in my first leadership position, I knew what football team everyone followed. It didn't take much for me to turn on *SportsCenter* on Monday morning and catch what those guys said about the Giants game or the Broncos game. Then at our Monday morning staff meeting I would say, "Wow, the Broncos looked good yesterday!" Or "Man, the Giants are really up and down this year." We'd probably spend a good five to seven minutes every Monday morning talking about the Sunday games or what was going to happen that night. I'd walk around and ask about kids' birthday parties, vacations, house projects. I obviously had to know about these things, but when someone told me their daughter was turning nine that weekend, I could ask on Monday how the party went.

Later on in my career, I took a management job at another location where I didn't really know anyone there and it was important for me to build these same relationships. One woman on my team was becoming a grandmother. Unfortunately her grandson had some complications when the baby was born. The baby was born with a heart problem. She told me what was going on and that she was going to be missing some work, adjusting her work schedule, etc. She needed to take time off to watch her other grandchildren so the parents could be in the hospital with the newborn. Of course I was willing to help her in any way possible; I fully supported her in her alternate work schedules. She did her part by working long days when she could so her task would get done and wouldn't affect others. She eventually went part time to support her family, and I supported that as well. When she was in the office, I'd ask how things were going. I wasn't prying, but I know she was stressed dealing with a sick grandchild. She'd give me the latest update, usually including an uplifting story about the granddaughter she was watching. This was important to her and she later contrasted this experience with that of a previous manager who didn't take the time to show compassion when she was dealing with the death of her father.

Loyalty

The act of constant visualization impresses upon or trains the subconscious mind. By training the subconscious mind you are developing and setting the rules and guiding principles that will dictate future decisions. If you constantly think selfish thoughts, when confronted with a situation where you have to make a decision, you will be driven to decisions that benefit you and may not always benefit those around you. This is a destructive behavior because it will destroy loyalty among you and those you depend on, such as friends, coworkers, and family.

If you are constantly thinking kind and generous thoughts, when confronted with a situation where you have to make a decision you will be driven to decisions that benefit all those around you. This is known as a win-win situation and goes a long way to building loyalty with those you depend on, such as friends, coworkers, and family.

Let us explore this a little further: When you make decisions that have positive effects on those around you, you set that example and create a culture that is inclusive, beneficial, and enjoyable for everyone around you. You will put out a good "vibe." I say this creates loyalty and therefore the people you surround yourself with will eventually be driven to make mutually beneficial decisions. You will create a network and culture of people who instinctively make win-win decisions. That is the foundation of building loyalty through loyalty.

In my own life, I have tried to create a culture of loyalty through loyalty when as a leader I would always strive to put the best interests of my team members at the forefront of my decision process. I was successful in making decisions for the employee that were beneficial for both the employee and the company. I never put one concern over the other. At times this would cause tension because in the short term it may not have been obvious that I had both parties' interests in mind; however, I can say that without any doubt my decisions allowed the company to be successful and at the same time I was effective in developing more loyalty among the employees that later would benefit the company by increasing the retention rate of some high-potential employees.

Here is one specific example of when I was looking out for an employee: I had a high-potential junior engineer on my staff. He was a driven individual and wanted to maximize his own potential. He signed up and was selected for a development program in our company designed to help people like him rise through the technical ranks. This opportunity only came around once a year, and the selection process was very stringent; they only wanted top performers. The program consisted of a series of four- to six-month assignments designed to get the employee exposure and experiences that might not have been readily available to the individual.

At the time he was about to embark on these series of rotations, his name came up as a good candidate to fill a role on a specific program. The program was struggling, and the guy on my staff had some experience that could fill a need on the program. He and I discussed the opportunity and he met with the program. Shortly after, he realized that he was indeed capable of filling the need for the struggling program; however, this wasn't going to be a stretch for him and would actually regress in his development. He would be going back to doing something he'd done several years before. This was opposite of the intent of the development program he was accepted to.

I was in the middle here, and I knew that taking this job wasn't in the best interest of this particular employee; however, I knew that if the company didn't succeed and lost money on that program it would have an indirect effect on all of us. When in this situation I would talk very openly with my employee, saying that I would push back on my management about him being the right person for the job; on the other hand I had to tell him that at times we need to look out for the company. It would have been much easier for me, and caused less grief for me, if I had just told him that he needed to take this assignment. Instead, I went to my boss and made the case that we needed to find someone else. The skill set wasn't unique enough that there wouldn't be someone else able to fill the role; it was just a matter of finding that person. I went out on a limb for my direct employee, and for a short time I was at odds with my boss. I was willing to do this because in my opinion, if my employee knew that someone was actually looking out for him, he would be likely to stay at the company. I had once quit my job because my boss wasn't looking out for his employees, and I didn't want to be the cause of someone, especially a high-potential employee, leaving the company. In the end it all worked out, and my boss and I were able to find someone else to fill that position, and my direct report was able to participate in the development program. He is still with the company and making positive contributions to the programs he is working on.

Engagement

One of the latest buzzwords at many companies is "engagement." At one company it was talked about, used as leverage against management in performance reviews, and used as a punch line during after-work happy hours. The Gallup organization was paid to come in and administer a survey to be used as a metric for measuring the level of engagement of the employees. In my opinion many in the company leadership completely missed the point of employee engagement. The word "engagement" was no longer a buzzword; it's become a chore. What was even worse is that we make excuses for it for not focusing on it: we do not have money to implement that, we do not have time to complete our action plans, the issues causing a lack of engagement are outside of my control.

There is a lot of research that explains why employee engagement is important to the performance of a company. Engaged employees tend to have less absenteeism, lower turnover, and higher productivity, which translates to higher profit margins for the company. I understand this because at times I've been not very engaged with my work, and when this happens I tend to procrastinate, and I am not nearly as efficient as I could be. In these instances, it will take me longer to complete a task than if I were really interested in completing the task. Let's just say that when I was inefficient, I wasted one hour a week in low productivity. Now if we extrapolate that to fifty employees, a hundred employees, or even a thousand, those hours can really add up each week. It's no wonder why companies find engagement important.

Improving morale or engagement is something basic and really does not need specific action plans or surveys to accomplish. It does not have to be a chore! Cultivating and creating a motivated workforce is something that leaders should be doing every day. Some simple examples leaders can do on a daily basis are to listen to your team members and genuinely be interested in them. One colleague I used to work with kept an action item list for his team so when someone on his team made a suggestion for improvement (or even made a casual complaint), he used this list to take an action and raise the concern to someone who could help. By creating that list, following through on the actions, and showing his team the progress made to resolve these issues, his team knew that someone was trying to make a difference. Again, these are the things that build loyalty. This colleague actively showed his team members that their opinions and concerns were valid and were worth taking action to resolve.

Based on the results of the Gallup survey, we would be required to create action plans with our teams. When I was required to perform action plans, I was determined to take actions that were going to be beneficial to the team and actually have a positive impact on the culture within my team and those we interacted with. It took me a while to realize this, but at first I had 15 people on my direct staff. With those 15 people, I might have had 5 that were passionate about a specific action plan. I might have five more that were passionate about other things, and five that maybe didn't feel as passionate about anything. We would have a few items on the table, and as a group try to come up with a consensus. Inevitably the five that were passionate about one topic and the five that were basically indifferent would all agree to one topic, leaving the remaining five forced to comply. The following year, I would realize that our action plans did nothing to improve our scores. Why? I might have had five people that did see some results and were happy with what was accomplished. But there were ten other team members that either were forced to comply or not really excited about the topic. And to make it worse, I probably made those who were forced to comply feel alienated from the group, as if their concerns were not valid for some reason.

Eventually I decided that approach was not going to get the desired results, and finally I took a different approach. At this time I had 12 people in my group, and I decided I would do 12 plans, as long as everyone owned the plan and it was something they thought was important. If someone on my team feels like they are recognized enough, there is no reason to have them on a recognition action plan; it won't move the needle for that person. I was able to achieve a dramatic increase in the scores for my team and was able to build a sense of loyalty within the group. Everyone felt that their concerns were valid and worth taking action.

Rewards

Anyone with children knows that when you reward children for the behavior you want them to emulate you will create more of that behavior. For example, in my house, if my kids get all their homework done for the week and are generally good (which is subjective) they are rewarded with ice cream on the weekends.

The same philosophy applies to managing a team. When the team does something you think is important it is important that you immediately reward that action. Most companies have reward programs, usually focused on some sort of monetary reinforcement. Most companies I have worked with would have some sort of rewards program where employees may be rewarded with cash or gift certificates. Some companies offer stock options or bonuses based on performance. These are good and powerful tools if used appropriately. They are most effective when issued in a timely manner.

When I saw someone go the extra mile in helping someone I would highlight that in a staff meeting. This reinforced my saying that this particular action was important to me and is encouraged. When it wasn't practical or I was unable to offer a monetary award, I would buy lunch for the team, or I would bring in a homemade baked good to share with the team. By rewarding the actions I thought were important, I would soon see more of that action. I don't know if people consciously made the decision to do these things, but the recognition I provided helped to program the subconscious of my team members. The reward would create a feeling of satisfaction, and eventually I would create a craving for that success (and probably sugar!).

A team leader should use any and all ways at their disposal to recognize and reward those that adopt and take action on the values and principles they think are important in driving success in their organization.

Accountability

Accountability is one of the building blocks for building trust, and when building teams, trust is the currency that drives success. As the leader building trust starts with you, you must hold yourself accountable in order to expect the same from those around you. Accountability is an odd concept because free will prevents anyone from forcing someone else to do anything they do not want to do; you simply cannot force someone to perform for you if they don't want to perform. Now, that is not to say that intimidation and threats do not produce some results, but these results are usually short lived. Sustained success is never achieved through intimidation and threats. Therefore I think we can all agree that intimidation and threats are not proper motivators. The key is to get people to want to be successful, and these people will hold themselves accountable.

Holding people accountable, including yourself, means not accepting excuses. Typically excuses on an individual basis can sound like reasons, but in the aggregate they become excuses. If you have ever known anyone who his habitually late they always have a reason for it. There was an accident on the freeway. My car had a flat tire. My kid was sick this morning. When you look at those reasons on an individual basis any one of them would be an acceptable reason for not being on time, but when being late becomes the norm, rather than the exception, these are excuses. In reality we all know that the reason the person is late is because they didn't make it a priority to get to work on time or to get to the meeting on time. Whatever they were doing before your appointment was more important than ensuring that they were on time.

Although you can create an environment where people hold themselves accountable, that does not mean that you can just give direction and walk away. One of the biggest tools at a leader's disposal is to follow through. By following through you send the signal that the task you assigned someone is important to you, and at the same time it shows that you care about their personal success.

Free Lunch

We all know you can't get something for nothing, and maximizing your potential and achieving your dreams is no different. A farmer works in the spring to prepare his grounds and planting seeds. Then the farmer waits until fall for the field to produce food. The farmer does not know how well the crop will turn out, but the farmer does know that if the work is put in up front and done right, he will reap the rewards in the fall. The same truths hold true with maximizing your potential. Time is a limited resource, and if you are spending your time pursuing your goals, something has to give. You may have to stay up late or get up extra early, causing you to sacrifice some sleep, or you may have to work while on vacation, on holidays, or weekends. In the end something has to give. In working to maximize my own potential, I have been required to sacrifice all those things mentioned. I do this because I know the time I invest in working on the things I need to do to get better will provide benefits in the long run.

Many professionals spend years in school achieving a bachelor's degree or higher. An engineer will spend four to five years studying, doing research, and spending time in the lab to get a degree. This is a lot of work and this is the case for most professions. All engineering students go through school and make these sacrifices because they have an expectation that the time they invest will pay off with a well-paying and meaningful job after graduation. We learn in school, whether it is high school, college, or graduate school, that we need to put in the work to be able to achieve good grades, and the harder we work the better our scores.

Eventually we get out in the "real world" and start on our careers. For some reason we get so focused on doing our jobs that we don't typically go that extra mile. Sure, we may be engaged in our work and give some extra discretionary effort, but even that is limited. In order to rise to the top, to maximize your potential, you have to be willing to go the extra mile for yourself. Going the extra mile means learning about your profession or trade beyond the training that your company provides. Spending a portion of your free time studying the newest theories and techniques, learning what your competitors are doing, and most important studying what your industry leaders are doing. I promise you one thing: the leaders in your profession are not the same individuals who are doing what everyone else is doing. They take time to continuously improve, and it is the extra hard work that will put you over the edge. If you do what everyone else is doing, then you will get the same results as everyone else. It can't happen any other way.

If you want to have a team that gets results that no other team can accomplish, you have to inspire them and teach them to go above and beyond. I am somewhat of a history fan, and I often find myself watching war movies, specifically of the World War II genre. One of my favorites is the HBO miniseries *Band of Brothers*. I recommend this series to anyone who wants to understand what it truly means to look out for the person sitting next to you, and to do your part so the team can be successful. *Band of Brothers* is the story of Easy Company of the US Army 101st Airborne division, and the series starts with Easy Company during their training. They had the toughest commanding officer in the Airborne division, and the troops hated it. They showed other companies heading out with a weekend pass, while Easy Company was spending the weekend running and training. However, as the war progresses, and Easy Company come in conflict with the enemy, it becomes clear that they are the best-trained company and as a result gained a reputation as being the most effective. They gained their reputation because they did the work necessary to be the best.

CHAPTER 9
Challenges

I have not failed. I've just found 10,000 ways that won't work.
—Thomas A. Edison

FROM TIME TO time on the journey to maximizing your potential you will find that a course of action or a decision you made didn't yield the results you were hoping for. It is at this point when you may be tempted to give up, go back to what you know, and settle back into your old habits. In other words, you will be tempted to accept your previous level of success and may even rationalize it by finding some of the highlights of that lifestyle.

Do not look at a setback as a failure or an indication that you do not have a higher potential available. When you set out to maximize your potential, you will start with a vision and make a plan to achieve that vision. You will set goals along the way to achieve the level of success you impressed upon your subconscious mind, and, yes, from time to time you will fall short of that goal. This should not be a discouragement, but a setback should be treated as a learning opportunity. In Colin Powell's book *It Worked for Me* he talks about having post-action meetings, and the purpose of these meetings was to review a past exercise, to evaluate what went right and what went wrong. This is a powerful exercise for maximizing our potential. As you set goals to achieve your vision it is wise from time to time to evaluate how you are doing against those goals. Are you taking actions that help achieve those goals, and most importantly, when you fall short are you learning from the mistakes and making adjustments to your plan so you can still move forward in achieving your decision?

Fear

When our founding fathers signed the Declaration of Independence this took tremendous courage because what they were doing by declaring independence from the king and establishing a free and independent country was considered treason and was punishable by death. These 56 men, by signing their names to this document, clearly and quite literally were signing their own death warrants if the revolution had failed. These men clearly understood the significance of signing the document; as Benjamin Franklin was quoted as saying, "We must all hang together, or assuredly we shall all hang separately."

Now, I am quite certain that most of us are not setting goals that amount to starting a new country, and the risks involved are not likely to require us to sign our own death warrant. However, fear is often the cause of us holding back from achieving success. Many of us are comfortable with the life we are living. We may not like the outcome of our lives, or we may dream of a better life, but we know how to live in our present circumstances with our present results. We are able to survive, and the thought of going for more, the thought of taking a risk, and introducing the possibility of a greater struggle will often times prevent us from moving forward to reach our potential.

The fear of the unknown will often drive us to accept results in our lives that we don't necessarily like. It is like that saying, "It is better to go with the devil you know rather than the devil you don't." It is our paradigm that causes the fear. Our paradigm only understands one reality and will cause discomfort and anxiety when we make a decision do something that conflicts with the paradigm. This is when you begin to rationalize and make excuses.

I grew up in the middle of nowhere in Illinois surrounded by cornfields. My friends were great guys, but very few of them really had much ambition other than having a good time as often as possible. Most of us worked at the same pizza place, and after work we'd all go to the same parties. So we worked, lived, and hung out together. There weren't many jobs around, and most of us were destined to work construction—hard backbreaking work that is fine when you are 20 but wears you down as you get older.

The fall after I graduated high school I had signed up for classes at a local junior college. I really didn't have any desire to go to school but my programming, my paradigm, led me to believe that was expected of me. A classmate of mine from high school and I were both still living at home at this point and we'd drive to the school but wouldn't go to class. About halfway through the first semester we both quit pretending and just stopped going to school altogether.

A few months later I was sitting in the house that three of us were subleasing from the owner of the pizza place where we all worked. It was one of those houses that was decorated in the early '70s and hadn't been updated in the roughly 20 years since. It had orange, brown, and white shag carpet that remained nasty no matter what we did to clean it. We had a couch that was missing slats, so if you sat in the wrong spot you would fall through. Our coffee tables were old wiring spools, and someone took the cap off the water main down the street to use as an ashtray. The thing weighed 15 pounds, so I guess we didn't have to worry about anyone walking off with it.

On one particular day, I was at home just watching TV and drinking some beers. One of my roommates came home and had taken some LSD. He was tripping on LSD, rolling joints for fun and drinking a bottle of Southern Comfort. It was at this moment that I decided to take responsibility for my own destiny, and from there my life immediately got better. The next day I went to the Navy recruiter and enlisted.

Now, I knew in my rational mind that the decisions I had been making weren't going to get me where I wanted to go in life. I could see that I was going down a dead-end road, which was not going to lead to a life of prosperity, of nice vacations, nice cars, or a comfortable life for a future family. I knew in my soul that I needed to join the Navy. I needed job training, I needed to change my environment, and I needed discipline, all of which the Navy was going to offer. However, even knowing all of that I was terrified walking into the recruiter's office. I remember having doubts when I signed the papers. The night before I left for boot camp, I couldn't sleep. This was something I needed to do, something I wanted to do, and I knew it was best for me, yet I was still scared. Even though I was making all the right decisions, my paradigm was resisting it. I didn't know it at the time, but I had to overcome the paradigm.

Overcoming the Paradigm

Because most of the fear will be caused by your paradigm, and the further you are reaching outside your comfort zone, the more struggle it will be to overcome your paradigm. The greater the stretch, the more resistance you'll find coming from your paradigm. Your paradigm is actually a good measuring stick for how far you are stretching yourself. When you set a goal and take action to achieve that goal, if you are not uncomfortable, your goal isn't really a stretch. For example, I mentioned earlier in this book that oftentimes in my career I would go for a promotion, but it was really just an extension of what I was already doing. When I moved into management, I was already leading teams; it seems that the title just came late. When I started leading bigger and bigger teams, it was really the same thing I was doing before, just with more people. They were stretches, but none of them really made me feel the fear and discomfort that I felt when I enlisted in the Navy. However, starting my company did make me more uncomfortable. I am often presented with ideas that I know are good for me, and I hesitate to take advantage of them. For example, there are some coaching programs that I am interested in participating in. I know that coaching is a valuable investment, assuming that the coach is good, but there is a significant amount of cost involved. I hesitate because if I invest the money into the coaching, I will be more likely to follow through with my business development and to leave the job I presently have. I know my paradigm is stopping me, telling me that it is a lot of money or causing me to feel doubt. My paradigm is comfortable with the life I presently have, and taking the risk puts everything I presently have in jeopardy—which is exactly why I am writing this book and starting my own business. I want to put this lifestyle in the past and replace it with a much better lifestyle, where my work is rewarding on a spiritual, emotional, and physical level. However, my paradigm resists that because it is contrary to my present conditions.

To overcome the paradigm, you first have to recognize it is the paradigm causing the fear. This is not always cut-and-dried; for example, you may have an instinctual nudge from your subconscious saying this isn't the time. You have to be able to distinguish between the two, and the more you deal with your paradigm, the more you'll begin to recognize the difference. Knowing is half the battle, so once you know that it is the paradigm that is causing your fear, through courage and determination you can overcome the paradigm. Remember, courage isn't a lack of fear but taking action in spite of your fear. Once you break through, you will establish a new paradigm and your new world will be comfortable, and then you will have to find another goal that makes you uncomfortable and break through that fear again!

Changing Cultures

A culture is essentially a group paradigm. Any time there is group of people who commonly gather there is a culture developed; your family, your work, your community all have a culture. When trying to maximize the potential of your team, you will likely have to overcome or change a culture. Changing your paradigm is a challenge in itself, but when trying to change a culture it is very much a struggle. Corporate CEOs spend careers trying to change corporate cultures, and the larger the corporation, the more challenging the culture is to overcome. I have seen and heard stories of people who have been working at a particular company for a long time and still resist change because they were trained to do a task a certain way more than 30 years ago, and they honestly believe that because it worked then it'll work now. This illustrates some of the challenges that come with changing cultures. Yet culture changes can be accomplished.

We have discussed some of the barriers in terms of your paradigm. One of the common barriers caused by your paradigm is complacency. Doing what is necessary to achieve a higher level of success is going to take work. We can all come up with reasons why we can't do more work and generally they are reasons why we can't invest the necessary time. For example, you can say you don't have time because of your children's activities. I say that if you truly evaluated what you do during the day, you can find time in your schedule to plan, study, read—whatever it is you need to do to become more successful. You'll have to form new habits to replace old habits, even if the habit is watching TV or hitting the snooze button in the morning. Personally, I often get up early before the rest of my family and while the house is quiet and before my day starts I take positive actions to help improve my condition. I find that is what works for me. My wife on the other hand likes to take advantage of the time after the kids go to bed; that is when she is able to concentrate on her tasks. There is always time in the day if we make it a priority to find the time and use it wisely.

The other reason I often hear is my spouse won't let me. And I have to ask why. Why wouldn't your spouse want you to achieve more in life, to achieve higher levels of success and to provide a better standard of living for the family? If your spouse truly doesn't want you to be successful, you may want to reconsider your relationship. I will assume, though, that this isn't the case so the problem is likely caused by their paradigms. This does present a challenge because not only do you have to push through your own fears, you will have to convince someone else to push through their fears as well.

When it comes down to it, you need to identify what the barriers are that are preventing you from being able to maximize your potential, and from there develop strategies that will allow you to overcome these barriers. I promise you that all the barriers that you identify can be overcome. The first thing to overcoming the barriers of your team members is to teach your team to overcome the barriers in their own mind. This can be challenging, because as a leader you need to convince your team that most of the barriers are truly in their own minds. You need to teach the team that because they haven't accomplished something in the past, that doesn't mean that they cannot accomplish it in the future, and that it only takes a different approach.

The second challenge to overcoming a complex barrier in the work place is overcoming the challenges of corporate culture. Oftentimes, especially with more senior employees, they get stuck on doing things the way they have always done it in the past. On some levels this does make sense: it is less risky to do what you know and what you are comfortable doing. You can attain predictable results, and the process is comfortable. But this goes against almost everything I've been talking about. Doing what you are comfortable with is the exact definition of being complacent. Complacency leads to mediocrity. Doing what was always done is not taking a risk, and nothing great or spectacular is accomplished without taking a risk. The Wright brothers took risks, Martin Luther King Jr. took risks, Rosa Parks took a risk, John Kennedy took a risk. All great things started by someone taking a risk. Lastly, by doing things the same way, even with minor adjustments, is standing still. I can promise you that if you are on top of your game today and continue to do the same things over and over, then your competitors will be looking for ways to do this better and will eventually surpass you in efficiency, cost, or performance in whatever product or service you are providing.

Checker Cabs used to be the image of a taxi in America. Checker pretty much only sold one vehicle, and that was the iconic yellow taxicabs. The body styles didn't really evolve much since their debut in 1958, and the company was complacent in selling one product. Because Checker did not have many updates since 1958, they no doubt had a good handle on the manufacturing process. They kept their cabs affordable by minimizing the retooling required to update their body styles every few years.

Checker did one thing and they did it well: they built taxicabs. However, Checker was stuck doing things the way it had always done business for more than 30 years. As time went on federal and state regulations changed and other cost-efficient options emerged to challenge Checker with products that were able to meet the needs of taxicab companies. Eventually, because of a lack of updates to their vehicles, Checker eventually closed its doors. Checker went out of business because of its culture, its complacency in doing things the way they had always been done, and as a result their competitors passed them by offering taxi drivers a more affordable solution, and Checker cabs are no longer the common sight in major cities that they once were.

I was given a leadership position at one time at an engineering company where there were a lot of senior engineers who were accustomed to doing work in a particular way. This culture originated when our company was pretty much the only game in town for a particular product line, and the company executives were friendly with the customers' executives, which made it easy to get contracts.

Also during this time the customer base had larger budgets and cost was less of a factor when awarding contracts. This lack of competition and focus on affordability caused a corporate culture where affordability wasn't part of the strategy. Fast forward several years, when competition grew, executives retired or moved to new positions, and there was a greater focus on affordability; the old way of doing business was no longer acceptable.

When I accepted that leadership position, I was an outsider, and therefore I did not have preconceived notions of how business was done in the past. So when I took over I decided I would articulate my vision of how things would be done, and how my direct reports would improve the overall quality and affordability of our products. When I first presented my ideas I would get some resistance, some blank stares, and some cynical comments. The overall reaction was that I wasn't going to be able to do what I wanted, and even if I did, it wasn't the way they did business so it wouldn't work. I wasn't discouraged, and I kept spreading my message. I didn't force anything; however, when I had an opportunity to influence how something would be done, I would do it. I eventually had some on the team buy in to my philosophies, and when they started seeing successes, they would share with their peers. Over time there was some change in the culture. I wasn't in that position long enough to see the full transformation; however, I was there long enough to see morale improve and productivity increase.

I believe I was successful in initiating a culture change because:

1. I lead by example. The attitudes and behaviors I wanted my team to possess, I possessed myself. I not only talked the talk but walked the walk.

2. I didn't force change, but through repetition I repeated the message. When there were questions and pushback, I

allowed everyone to have their say. However, when there was evidence of a culture change, I celebrated it. I recognized it in staff meetings and rewarded those who exemplified the characteristics I wanted.

3. I created allies in the culture change. I had members of my team who believed in the changes I wanted and helped push the ideas. Ideas coming from one's peers usually has more impact than from the top down, especially coming from me, someone who was considered an outsider when I showed up.

I was patient. I knew the changes I wanted to implement were not going to happen overnight, and if I forced them they wouldn't happen at all. Through my patience coupled with the strategies I already described, I was able to make changes in less than a year, which I think was just about as fast as I could have made them if I forced them.

Status Quo

"If you always do what you've always done, you'll always get what you've always got."
—Henry Ford

It is very easy to become complacent with our circumstances in life. I talked about habits earlier in the book, and in reality complacency is the habit of accepting our present results. In this case your habit can actually be hurting you and preventing you from maximizing your potential. Time does not stop for anyone, so by the very nature of things the world is moving forward. If you are not moving forward and all those around you are, you are essentially moving backwards.

To be an effective leader, you must always be looking to improve, and I mean improve everything.

A leader must strive to be the best in his particular field of expertise. I spent many years working in the engineering field, and I would like to think I was a successful leader of engineering teams. I never claimed to be an expert in any particular product that I worked on; however, I did make claims that I was an expert in leading technical teams. I certainly had to have domain knowledge of our products, and I have a technical background in the discipline I was leading, but I let the individuals working on the team be the experts. My job was to become better at leading teams, better at helping to resolve problems, and better at achieving the desired results. My field was engineering management, and I was committed to becoming an expert in that particular field.

If you were an engineer on my team, I would still expect you to learn and grow your skills. There are always new problems to solve and new innovations to be created. Those who worked on my team were pushed into stretch assignments to get new experiences and exposure. If anyone on my team was content doing what they were doing, in a short amount of time they would find their services no longer needed. That isn't to say I would necessarily fire them, but we'd have new challenges where innovative solutions would be required. Those that didn't adapt were soon adding little to no value and would be replaced by someone who was adding value.

Greatness is not achieved by standing still. Columbus didn't discover America by staying at home. Neil Armstrong didn't take "one small step for man, one giant leap for mankind" by being content as a Navy pilot. Barack Obama didn't become the first black president of the United States by being complacent as a community organizer in Chicago. All these men achieved what they did because they continued to push forward and refused to be complacent in their present circumstances.

Apple could be considered a top technology company, and they sell computers, laptops, tablets, MP3 players, and phones. Apple isn't complacent selling the products they have already produced; they spend a considerable amount of time and resources developing the next generation of their products. We can all admit that they wouldn't remain on top very long without developing new products.

Automobile manufacturers are another example of an entire industry that continuously looks for ways to improve their products. New cars have additional features and technology not available on previous models. They experiment with new materials to make vehicles safer for the passengers to increase the chance of survival in the event of an automobile accident. Automobile manufacturers are even looking for ways to improve fuel efficiency and other ways to reduce the cost of ownership. All these are ways that demonstrate that the automobile industry fights against complacency.

When I was a teenager, video rental stores were all over the place. I grew up in a town of around 2,500 people and we had two stores in our town. Blockbuster Video was the giant among video rental stores and was the place to go to rent a movie. The Blockbuster business model was to provide convenient locations in nearly every town for people to stop in, browse titles, and rent a video for a night or two. This model worked well, until Internet commerce really began to pick up. Then a company called Netflix came along and delivered movies to your mailbox. You could keep them as long as you wanted and when you returned them, they would send you another movie from your list. There was little to no hassle for the consumer with this business model. During this time Blockbuster was complacent being the giant in the home video rental business and did not make appropriate adjustments to its business model. Eventually it tried to get into the home delivery of movies but it was too little too late and Blockbuster eventually closed its doors. Had Blockbuster been proactive and not been complacent with its business model, it could have offered competition to Netflix and perhaps stayed in business. If you are complacent in your work and your business model, there is a competitor out there that is looking for a better way to do business. Continuous improvement and that determination to push forward is what will propel you to the top and keep you there.

CHAPTER 10
Find Your Purpose

LIFE IS NOT a series of random events that happen but a series of events that you cause to happen. By causing the events that happen to you in your life, by default you create the type of life you are living, whether it is beneficial or detrimental to your well-being.

It is true that you can't control what other people do, but you can control who you let into your life and to what extent their decisions influence your life. Obviously your spouse can have a great impact on your life and most people will agree with that. Even my eight-year-old son will tell me, "Happy wife, happy life." I don't know why he knows that but he is right. Although your spouse can impact your life, keep in mind it is your decision who to marry. People cannot have control over you unless you give them that control.

Individually we cannot influence the nation's economy. You can control your personal economy. You can control where you work, who you work for, what skills you develop, and to what extent you develop them. If you have a skill people need and you are good at your trade, you will be valuable. No matter what your line of work, if there is a need, even in tough times there is a market. Even in the great depression, there were still people of money and influence.

Tornados, hurricanes, earthquakes, and other tragic events happen, and cannot always be predicted or controlled. Obviously the easy thing to say is not to live in an area where tornados happen, but then you might live in an area prone to hurricanes. You do have some say in where you live, but most places on the globe are susceptible to some sort of natural disaster, and other tragic events can happen regardless of where you live. All of these things are survivable if you are prepared to respond when they happen and not just react. People in Oklahoma have storm shelters built into their homes, and when the tornado warnings sound people enter their shelters. People in Florida have storm shutters installed on their homes so they can protect their homes in the event of a hurricane. People in California have strict building codes to help their buildings withstand the impacts of an earthquake. Additionally, everyone can be prepared for what might happen, a plan to secure valuable documents, insurance information, and practice evacuation drills.

Don't Limit Yourself

The law of attraction simply states that what you think about you bring about. Whatever is dominating your thoughts is what you bring into your life. Before I'd even heard of the law of attraction we used to say that birds of a feather flock together. That was a way of saying that people of similar interests will somehow find each other. This happens through groups, sports teams, social clubs, and these days, social media. If you are a baseball fan, soon you will find

MAXIMIZING THE HUMAN POTENTIAL

someone at work who is also a baseball fan and will talk about last night's game, or the next season. That is one simplified effect of the law of attraction, but a good illustration of its reality and power.

Every great accomplishment started with a vision, and most likely an obsession. Thomas Edison was obsessed with creating an electric light bulb, Henry Ford was obsessed with creating a car for the common man, and John Kennedy had the great vision of putting a man on the moon and beating the Soviets in the space race. If you can dream it, you can do it. Whatever thought dominates your thinking, your actions will produce the results you are thinking about.

I have provided examples of great accomplishments in human history, and how thought and visualization caused them to happen. I have also given examples of how this has worked in my own life. Whether it was to be the best technician in the shop while I was in the Navy, the car I wanted in college, or the career path I wanted at my job, the thoughts that dominated my thinking produced the results I was thinking about.

Imagine this: if you truly do create the events that happen in your life just think for a moment about the power that you really do have over the circumstances in your life. Just think of the possibilities that are open to you if you really can create your own destiny.

With this newfound power over the universe, and most importantly your own destiny, the first thing to do is to set your vision and set it large. Olympic athletes don't go to the games with the intention just to finish. Professional sports teams don't start the season with the intention of finishing the season in last place. No, athletes of all kinds start off with the intention of being the best, winning the championship, or bringing home a gold medal. This is your life. It may be the only one you have, so why not set your expectation, vision, and goals to making the most of your life? Really, what do you have to lose? Make your vision to be the best of what you want your life to become. Visualize the absolute best of what makes you happy. Good enough is the enemy of great. Complacency is the engine that drives mediocrity. If life were a class in school, do not settle for a C but strive for the A.

I remember one night at the family dinner table when I was growing up, my father was trying to talk one of my sisters into learning to play golf. She dismissed the idea and my father replied with "Don't limit yourself." In hindsight that was good advice and became a standard response in the family every time someone was unwilling to try something. My sister did not take up golf at my father's request, but that phrase is still often uttered around the Thanksgiving table.

To give further credit to my father, one evening I was talking to him about what I was trying to accomplish with my life. I told him about plans for running a business, and at the time I was planning to purchase an existing business. He asked some questions about why I thought I would make a good business owner, and I told him some of the key attributes that I thought I had that would make a business successful. I told him about my ability to build and lead teams and help people achieve more than they thought they were capable of achieving. He then asked me why I didn't start a business focused on teaching people what I have already learned how to do. By focusing a business on teaching people to build better teams and develop leaders I could help more companies become successful, and as a result affect more lives than I could just running a single business. After some consideration, I realized that I was limiting myself and refocused my efforts.

The key to maximizing your potential is to expand your vision and to raise your expectations from life. You can and will only achieve what it is you expect, in other words what you believe you can achieve. Whatever you decide to do in life, decide to be the best.

Purpose

I am a firm believer that everyone has a purpose for their lives. Everyone has a skill or talent that they can use to contribute to society. How do you know what your purpose is? How do you know what talent you have to contribute to society? Usually you are drawn to activities that best utilize your skills. When you choose an activity that makes use of your talents you will find you have a natural talent, or knack for it if you will. You will be naturally drawn to the type of work for which you are best suited. If you like to build things with your hands, you may be drawn to construction. If you like to research and learn how the world works, you may be interested in teaching or engineering. If you are interested in helping the downtrodden you might be called to social work, clergy, or charity work. If you are interested in athletics, you may be called to being an athlete or a coach. Whatever it is you are drawn to, that is likely what your purpose is. When you find yourself doing something that you can do all day without getting tired, where time just flies by when you are doing it and you can't wait to do it again tomorrow, or when going to work on Monday morning becomes your favorite time of the week, you have found your purpose.

Once you find your true passion and purpose, pursue it with all of your passion and energy. Do not allow doubt to creep into your pursuit by limiting yourself with excuses like:

- My current career doesn't allow me to do that.
- How do I make money doing that?
- I can't make enough money to support my family doing that.

Well, let me tell you something that I have found to be true. There are successful people in all lines of work, from engineering to teaching to construction. Whatever your chosen profession, if you pursue your work with passion and energy, you can and will be successful both monetarily and spiritually.

Pride

When I am at an important meeting at work or watching someone give a presentation in front of a large crowd, I will often look at the person's shoes. Ironically I pay more attention to a man's shoes than I do a woman's shoes. This was a habit I probably picked up in the Navy, but I am looking to see if the person has a shine in his shoes, or if they are scuffed and ragged looking. To me this is an indicator of how much pride someone takes in their outward appearance. For most men, shoes are just something we put on as we walk out the door. Having the forethought to shine those shoes is attention to detail. I have been in situations where my wife and I would go to an event and underestimate the dress code. I immediately feel out of place when this happens and get upset for not knowing the dress code. I take pride in my appearance and would rather be overdressed than underdressed. If I find that I am overdressed, I can always take off my tie or jacket. No big deal. But if I find myself needing a jacket or tie and I don't have one, well I have to look like a fool.

In the movie *Patton* there is an early scene where General Patton shows up to his command in Africa after the Americans had just lost

MAXIMIZING THE HUMAN POTENTIAL

at Kasserine Pass in Tunisia. When surveying the crew, the general made this observation: "You want to know why this outfit got the hell kicked out of it? A blind man could spot it. They don't act like soldiers; they don't look like soldiers; why should they be expected to fight like soldiers?" I don't know if the general actually said this or this was just a line in the movie, but it brings home the point of having pride in your appearance. How you appear on the outside reflects how you feel on the inside. If you are a proud person, if you have respect for yourself and show that in your appearance by wearing clean clothes and keeping your hair neat and tidy, you project that pride to those whom you encounter every day. I have three children, a girl and two boys. It is important to me and my wife that when the children leave the house they are dressed appropriately, have clean clothes, and have well-kept hair. We make sure they take showers regularly and trim their fingernails. My wife and I also make sure that they have proper manners and etiquette when meeting new people or when they are in public places. As a result, we can take our children to restaurants and expect them to behave. We can take them to the store with us when we have to run errands. If my children look unkempt or dirty or misbehave in public, that is a direct reflection on us as parents. It shows that either these things were not important to us or that my wife and I lack the discipline to instill proper values into our children.

In the workplace, you should still take pride in your appearance. I know what you might be thinking: but I am a mechanic, I am covered in grease and oil all day. I understand; I have been known to dabble a little in auto mechanics myself. I completely understand that with almost every job there is dirt, grime, and grease just looking to get on your clothes, stain your skin, and get under your fingernails. Even wearing gloves I seem to get pretty dirty.

However, this doesn't mean you can't wash your clothes after work and wear clean clothes to work the next day. You can spend a little time cleaning your hands, arms, and under your fingernails before you go out for the evening. When you go to your kid's sports game or go out to for the evening, there is no reason to continue looking like you are still at work.

I worked as an engineer for many years. In the engineering profession, we often have two distinct work environments, the laboratory and the office. The dress code for both environments is often different, and the laboratory was often more relaxed in its dress code. For example, in the office the attire was business causal, meaning slacks and collared shirt. In the lab, typically jeans and a collared shirt, and if you were working second or third shift often T-shirts were acceptable. The differences in dress codes were typically understood and accepted. However, even on second and third shift there were standards. I had one engineer working for me, and this guy would show up every day with clothes on that looked like he pulled them out from the bottom of the clothes pile. The guy would wear jeans and a T-shirt to work, and for the life of me I could never figure out how they could get so wrinkled. I rarely find the need to iron jeans or T-shirts— in fact I wear them because they don't need to be ironed—but this guy would make them look horrible. The guys would come to my office and ask if I saw him today. It almost became some sort of joke. In the end I ended up saying something to his boss about his unprofessional appearance, and he eventually moved on, probably because realized he didn't fit in.

You've probably heard the expression to dress for the job you want, not the one you have. My takeaway here is to dress for the life you want, not the one you have. If you can't afford the nicest clothes, fine; wear the best you can afford and most importantly take care of the clothes you have.

You should take pride in the appearance of everything you do or own. You may not own the biggest, newest house, but you do live somewhere. Just because your house or apartment may be old, small, or outdated doesn't mean you can't take pride in your property. You can still keep it clean and tidy. Keeping clean paint on the walls and keeping your countertops and floors free from dust and clutter shows a level of pride in your home. On the outside of your home, you can keep your lawn trimmed and clean so when people drive by or walk by the appearance is pleasing. You may own an older vehicle, but you can still take it to the car wash and vacuum the interior. I have children so I know how messy a car can get, but you can still pick up the trash from snacks or vacuum when the kids get in with muddy feet.

These little things go a long way in helping you change your life. You may be thinking, how does keeping my car clean help me improve my life? How will a clean yard or a clean appearance change my life? Taking pride in the appearance of your clothes, home, and car will give you a feeling of satisfaction and impress upon your subconscious the importance these hold in your life. As a result, through the law of attraction you will continue to attract nice things into your life.

I've already discussed working to do your best, but let's take this one step further. One thing that I do not understand is when employees openly and at times aggressively complain about the workplace. They complain about management, or management complains about the unions, or somebody is complaining about a colleague or spouse. There is no productivity in this type of talk at all, and in fact that level of negativity reduces productivity. My father refers to this as "lunchroom talk," where the guys or gals get together at lunchtime to complain about this policy or that person.

Have you ever heard players of a championship sports team badmouth the coaches or ownership? Or a coach say that the team would win if the players just did what he told them to do? No, I am sure you haven't because that causes division in a team, and a team cannot fully operate in that type of environment, at least not with any level of sustained success.

The workplace is no different. All levels of employees need to be working toward the same goal. If you find yourself complaining about what is happening at your workplace, you might be part of the problem. There are some horrible places to work—I am sure that is true. I've had enough different experiences to know that a horrible boss can change the way you feel about your job. You can't always choose your boss, but you can always change the way you respond to your boss. Evaluate how you respond to a less than desirable boss. Do you complain and bring everyone down with you? Remember negativity breeds negativity. There are options; we do live in a free society. You can look for another position in your present company. In my company often management is rotated every two to three years, so you can always wait it out. Maybe you can work with your boss to make things better; in some cases he or she may not know there is a problem. I know I've had people approach me and offer advice on how I can approach things differently, and they were able to point out flaws in my attitude or demeanor. Finally, you can choose to work someplace else. If the culture of your company is truly that bad, it's probably a good idea to go someplace else, because companies that do not treat their employees well will not survive long.

Karma

Karma is believing that good or bad things happen to you as a result of good or bad actions you have taken. The idea of karma goes beyond just Hinduism and Buddhism and is a basic tenant of most religions. Good things happen to good people, and evil things happen to evil people. This is consistent with the premise of this book that life is not a series of random events that happen but a series of events that you cause to happen.

The world doesn't always seem perfect, and we can all think of times when someone did something evil and seemed to get away with it. If you believe in karma, you can rest assured that person got what was coming to them. Enron is an example of this. The top executives at Enron manipulated their balance sheets to make it look like they were more valuable than they actually were. Because they looked so good on paper, investors were willing to invest in Enron, and when it came time to pay back the loans, to those who invested, Enron simply couldn't pay. This is an example where someone, in this case Enron, was doing something unethical, and karma caught up with them.

Closing

Success will come through the absolute belief that privilege and abundance is achievable by everyone, and that these things are an inalienable right of the human condition. The meaning of life is not to get by with what we have, nor is the meaning of life to be complacent. The meaning of your life it to maximize your potential by going after your dreams and aligning your skills and talents to maximize your potential.

I talked about a moment in my life when I realized my life wasn't heading in the direction I wanted it to go and that is what caused me to join the Navy. Another dramatic decision in my life was when I decided to start my own company. My life was not going the way I wanted it to go, and I was once again becoming complacent. I decided that by writing this book and starting a company based on these teachings, I would be able to share these thoughts and ideas with many more people than I could by limiting myself to my circle of influence.

What is the moment that will cause you to want to change the trajectory of your life? Define what that moment is, define that life you want to live, create that vision in your mind and go after it. If you are saying that your life is good enough and that you are comfortable, then you are not achieving greatness. There are successful people in all callings, and these are the people who never stop learning and collecting the knowledge needed to achieve their maximum potential.

If you have the ability and wherewithal to read and comprehend the ideas presented in this book, you have the mental capability to change your mental programming. Remember that your reality, your paradigm, has been programmed into your subconscious mind, by what your conscious mind has allowed to pass. You can reprogram your subconscious mind by repetitively focusing on the reality you want. If you want to be a successful doctor, picture yourself as a doctor. Picture graduating medical school and what your medical practice may look like. Picture the people you will help in your profession. If you want to be a teacher, picture the children in your classes learning and getting excited about the topics you teach. Picture the positive influence you intend to have on your students' lives.

Create a vision of your life in words and pictures. Dr. Joseph Parent, the author of *Zen Golf*, describes the importance of seeing your golf shot before you hit it. He says players should picture the shot from the beginning of the swing through the result. The golfer Jason Day is a classic example of someone who does this because before every shot, he will literally close his eyes to picture the shot in his mind. Dr. Parent will give this advice to his students and they will often respond by saying they are not very good at creating pictures in their mind. Dr. Parent will ask them to tell them what the shot will do, and they will describe how they want the ball to travel and what the result would be. It is at that point Dr. Parent will enlighten the student by saying that is a vision of the shot.

If you cannot see pictures in your mind, write down in detail what your vision of success looks like. Once you do that, read it out loud over and over and over, and I promise if you do that your mind will eventually create the picture you are struggling to see. Dream the picture then live the dream.

Imagine life as an opportunity for continuous improvement. If given the choice at birth you would not say you wanted to finish life in the middle of the pack. You would say that you want to win at life, and why wouldn't you? Life is a whole lot easier when you are successful. Sure, having money and affluence does not mean that there are not challenges in life, but it changes things when you do not have to spend time and energy deciding where your next meal is coming from or wondering if your car will make it through the winter. Fight the desire to become complacent in your surroundings. Fight the desire to accept the reality that has been programmed into your mind, and live your life as if there is a championship ring on the line.

The SEC requires funds to tell investors that a fund's past performance does not necessarily predict future results. The statement from the SEC is correct; similarly, when investing in the human potential present thinking does necessarily predict future results. Life is not a series of events that happen to you but a series of events you cause to happen! You can change your future simply by changing the way you think, which will in turn change the programming in your subconscious mind.

Sustained greatness and success always comes from great leadership. This is why you can go to any bookstore and see books on leadership written by sports coaches who are known to have successful dynasties during their tenure. These people understand the value of leadership and want to share their experiences with others so they might be able to achieve the same successes. I guess this is why these people are coaches: they always want to help others succeed, be it in basketball, football, or in another line of work.

Leadership is important because no one person can acquire all the knowledge they need to achieve the highest levels of success. Great sales people need a back office for support. Doctors rely on an office staff and nurses. Business managers rely on help from lawyers, accountants, and financial analysts. You will need to build your team and get them working toward the same goal. To get everyone working toward the same goal you need to articulate your vision clearly and with confidence. Present to your team a vision of a future that is better than the one they already envision. Give your team a sense of optimism that their best days are in front of them, and you will help them get there.

Create goals to achieve your vision. Your goals and vision should be large and outside your comfort zone. Your comfort zone is a boundary set up by your conscious mind. When you receive that intuitive push to go after something, that push is your subconscious mind inspiring you. If your vision is aligned with your talents, then you are guaranteed success. Great success comes from taking risks and putting yourself out there. Sure, at times there will be some setbacks, and it will look like failure, but these are learning experiences. Each time you reach or fail to reach a goal on your journey to success, take time to reflect on that last leg of the journey. Contemplate and internalize the events that went right and why, as well as the things that did not go as well as you had hoped. These are learning opportunities that life has presented for you to grow from.

Develop a plan to achieve your vision of success. What milestones do you need to achieve along the way? Do you need education, experiences, knowledge, or a mentor? These things are milestones that you should have in your plan, as well as what steps are needed to achieve these milestones. Always keep in mind that the planning phase is extremely important, even if your plan is not perfectly executed. Planning is so important that anyone looking for a business loan is always asked for a business plan. The business plan is important because it shows to the investors that you have put some thought into your business and understand what it will take to execute your business. Investors know that your plan will not be executed exactly as outlined in the document, but they want to know that you have thought about and understand the environment, limitations, and realities of your business.

When creating the plan to maximize your potential, it is important that you think about what you are willing to do to achieve your goal. Your plan should outline what type of time commitment you are willing to make. If you need more education or some sort of experience you are not able to achieve in your present life, these things take a commitment. Oftentimes this means sacrificing something, like putting your bowling league on hold for a few years while you finish your education, or waiting to buy that new car until you finish paying for the classes or certification you may need to seek. Remember a sacrifice is giving up something of lesser value to achieve something of greater value in the future.

Finally and probably most importantly, always and actively show gratitude. There is a reason that we teach our children to say thank you when someone does something for them. Gratitude is a powerful emotion for both the giver and recipient. By truly showing gratitude for what you have, you are actually programming your mind to achieve more of what you are grateful for. Emotion mixed with thought accelerates the programming process. If you show gratitude for the car you have, your subconscious mind will try to bring about more and better cars. If you show gratitude for the people in your life, you will attract more people with those traits.

Also we have all been on the receiving side of someone who was grateful for something we did for them. It could be as simple as holding a door for someone, giving some key piece of advice, or helping a family member through a time of need. When people show appreciation or gratitude to us it makes us feel better and in turn causes us to want to do more of those actions that make us feel good. So it is logical that if we show true gratitude to someone who helped us, they will feel good about what they have done and will continue to produce those same actions.

You can make your life into something—anything—you want it to be. Your life is a series of events created by you: why not create a series of events that will lead you to be prosperous, healthy, wealthy, and most of all happy?

ANDREW SHAFFER has devoted more than 20-years in various leadership roles helping his colleagues and direct reports to efficiently and effectively direct their efforts toward accomplishing their desired results. Andrew found his greatest job satisfaction was derived from helping others achieve next level success, whether it was through mentorship, training, or by setting an example of good leadership. He started a consulting business with the exclusive purpose of helping other leaders develop the skills required to create dramatic leaps in their personal success, and to help leaders build effective teams that produce successful results year after year.

SHAFFERINGENUITY.COM

www.ingramcontent.com/pod-product-compliance
Lightning Source LLC
Chambersburg PA
CBHW021542200526
45163CB00014B/787